DIARY AT 50

THE TIMES

DIARY AT 50

THE ANTIDOTE TO THE NEWS

Patrick Kidd

Published by Times Books

An imprint of HarperCollins Publishers
Westerhill Road
Bishopbriggs
Glasgow G64 2QT
www.harpercollins.co.uk
times.books@harpercollins.co.uk

First edition 2016

© Times Newspapers Ltd 2016
www.thetimes.co.uk

The Times® is a registered trademark of Times Newspapers Ltd

The contents of this publication are believed correct at the time of printing.
Nevertheless the publisher can accept no responsibility for errors or omissions,
changes in the detail given or for any expense or loss thereby caused.

HarperCollins does not warrant that any website mentioned in this title will
be provided uninterrupted, that any website will be error free, that defects will
be corrected, or that the website or the server that makes it available are free
of viruses or bugs. For full terms and conditions please refer to the site terms
provided on the website.

A catalogue record for this book is available from the British Library.

ISBN 978-0-00-820552-2

10 9 8 7 6 5 4 3 2 1

Printed and bound in Great Britain by Clays Ltd., St Ives plc.

MIX
Paper from
responsible sources
FSC **FSC™ C007454**
www.fsc.org

FSC™ is a non-profit international organisation established to promote the
responsible management of the world's forests. Products carrying the FSC
label are independently certified to assure consumers that they come from
forests that are managed to meet the social, economic and ecological needs
of present and future generations, and other controlled sources.

Find out more about HarperCollins and the environment at
www.harpercollins.co.uk/green

CONTENTS

Introduction	7
Acknowledgements	16
Court in the act	17
Film and television	23
Crime and punishment	31
Apt names	37
The power and the Tory	41
Short and sweet	53
Sex	57
Errors	65
Local politics	73
Fortunes of war	79
On the left	85
Scotland, Wales and Ireland	95
Embarrassments	101
Health	109
Sport	115
Europe	121
Liberals and other party animals	127
Americans	135
Foreign policy	143

Books and authors 151

Food and drink 159

The media 165

The royal family 171

On stage 177

Religion 189

Commons people 197

Music 203

Peers 211

Animals 217

Speaking collectively 223

Explorers 227

Planes, trains and automobiles 233

Whitehall 239

The last post 245

And finally... 249

INTRODUCTION

Let's start with the dead guillemots.

One of my favourite *Times* Diary stories never appeared in the newspaper, nor was it even true, but it sums up what the column is about. Picture the scene: a slow summer's day around the turn of the millennium, not much happening in the traditional hunting grounds for diarists. The politicians have long fled Westminster, the summer parties and book launches have fizzled out, everyone interesting is on holiday. And the Diarist of the time has a stinking hangover and is running late for morning conference.

Conference is the 11am gathering of all the section editors on the newspaper, where they present their rough plan for the day. In those days, the Diary editor was expected to attend and present a few amusements to round off the meeting, a sort of "And finally" piece of light relief. The Diarist's main role is as court jester to the king. Sometimes it falls flat: one predecessor still shudders at the memory of being called on at the end of conference and starting to explain a story that he quickly realised wasn't as funny or as interesting as it had seemed outside the room. When he reached the punchline there was a silence before the Editor just snarled: "Pathetic."

Anyway, the guillemots. The Diarist had a sore head, his team hadn't found any stories the night before, the cupboard was bare and he was off to the editor. Yet an hour later, back he skipped with a smile on his face and a song in his heart. "Got away with it," he said.

His lackeys were puzzled. *How* did you get away with it? "I told them the story about the dead guillemots," he replied. "Emma Nicholson keeps finding corpses of seabirds on her back garden, one a day for the past month. She thinks that someone is playing a prank on her."

7

"Where did you hear that?" his deputy asked him. "Oh, it's not true," the Diarist said casually, "but they loved it and it bought us a few hours to find something that is true". Sure enough, when he attended the afternoon conference, when fuller plans must be presented, they had scraped together a passable column. "What happened to the guillemots?" the Editor asked him. "Couldn't stand it up," the Diarist replied.

The thing about the guillemot story is that it could have been true and if it had been – we do, generally, try to check that a tip has some vague basis in fact – it would have been an excellent Diary item, combining a famous name with an absurd situation. The column is there mainly to provide amusement or something that the readers didn't know. Its aim, certainly in my time as Diarist and for much of its history, was to raise an eyebrow or a chuckle. The column is the antidote to the gloom on the rest of the news pages.

The Times was late to getting a Diary column. The *Evening Standard*'s Londoner's Diary was founded in 1916 (an antidote to war, perhaps) and presented its readers with political gossip and upper-crust tittle-tattle, satirised brilliantly by Evelyn Waugh in *Vile Bodies*. The only thing worse than appearing in the column, so they said, was not appearing in it. There is a wonderful story about the young John Betjeman, who worked for a while as a junior diarist on the Standard, running into the editor's office and saying: "Please, sir, I think I've got one of those scoop things!" His boss asked how he was sure. "Well," the future poet laureate said. "I've rung the *Evening News* and they haven't got it."

Other papers soon followed suit, notably the William Hickey column in the *Express*, established by Tom Driberg in 1933 and named after an 18th-century diarist. The historian David Kynaston called Driberg "the founder of the modern gossip column", while Driberg himself said the column was "an intimate biographical column about men and women who matter". He often used it to plug his mates, including Waugh.

While *The Sunday Times* had long had its Atticus column, which was written in the early 1950s by Ian Fleming, creator of the James Bond books, the daily *Times*, at that stage under different ownership, did not get a Diary or similar sort of gossip column until the mid-1960s. Perhaps it was felt that the Paper of Record did not merit such frippery.

May 3, 1966, was a day of great change for the paper. In a revolutionary move, the front page, until then covered in small classified adverts, finally had news stories placed on it. Since 1952, when *The Manchester Guardian* took the plunge, *The Times* had been the last national newspaper not to promote the news. "We hope that any inconvenience the unfamiliar look of today's issue may cause will be short lived," the leading article said.

Among the other changes was the introduction of a Diary column on the leader page. This clearly had caused the Editor, Sir William Haley, some concern. "Some readers have been alarmed by reports that it is to be a gossip column," he wrote, noting that there had also been vehement objection from readers to the introduction of a crossword in 1930. "Some people have expressed the dark suspicion," he went on, "that one of the reasons *The Times* is modernising itself is to get more readers. Of course it is."

The Diary appeared under the title "As It Happens". This was the result of a competition among the staff, with the Editor offering a prize for the best name. Out of the many entries submitted, the winning one was thought up by … Sir William Haley. It did not last. Before its first anniversary, the column was renamed as The *Times* Diary and signed by PHS, a reference to Printing House Square, the address off Fleet Street where the paper was based.

9

There was little scandal to concern the readers. The first item was a report showing that the Leaning Tower of Pisa was also rotating very slowly. There were also stories about a charity arts sale at Sotheby's, why the mayor of New York's signature keeps changing ("I have different moods"), a concern that Dartmoor ponies were being sold abroad for veal and, the best item, the placing of a memorial seat for Frank Benson, the Shakespearean actor, with an anecdote about his organisation of an actors' cricket team, which regularly featured actresses. "To be stumped at Old Trafford by Ophelia," the Diarist reported, "is an experience which would have been impossible but for Benson."

The first Times Diarist was Roger Berthoud, who had formerly worked on the *Standard's* Diary, where he got the scoop on General De Gaulle's view of the Profumo affair: "That will teach the English to try and behave like Frenchmen." He was succeeded in 1969 by Ion Trewin, who went on to earn distinction as the paper's literary editor and administrator of the Booker Prize. In 1972, Michael Leapman took on the column, writing it for five years and delighting readers, when stories were thin on the ground, with tales from his allotment.

Between 1978-81, including the year when *The Times* was closed by industrial action, the Diary had a daily theme – London Diary, Arts Diary, Sports Diary and so on – and was written by a different author each day, but the stories were of a similar style to the PHS columns. One of those who got their break through writing the column at this time was Joseph Connolly, now author of a dozen comic novels, who owned a bookshop in Hampstead at the time and complained to a customer about being bored by the Sports Diary. "Would you like to write a Books Diary?" asked the customer, who turned out to be Peter Stothard, then the newspaper's comment editor, and so Connolly came on board.

When Harold Evans became Editor of *The Times* in 1981, he restored a dedicated Diary editor. Peter Watson and Robin Young held the post before Penny Perrick, in 1983, became the first woman to write the column. She was followed by Angela Gordon and Rosemary Unsworth. They were based at the time in an old rum warehouse in Wapping and alcohol formed a significant part of the Diarist's life. The three-hour lunch with contacts, returning half an hour before afternoon conference, was followed by evenings at social parties. Nor was boozing the sole preserve of the Diary. Unsworth recalls her desk being near the business team and finding her work disturbed by snoring coming from the deputy business editor, who would sleep off a heavy session beneath his desk. "He went on to become a very rich investment banker," she told me.

In 1988, the Diary returned again to being written by different hands for each day of the week, including Alan Coren, Clement Freud and Simon Barnes, but this was again short-lived and Nigel Williamson took over in 1990 as Diary editor. It was just after this that David Cameron made his first appearance in the column in a piece speculating on changes to John Major's kitchen cabinet. The prime minister's political secretary, Judith Chaplin, wanted to spend more time in the Newbury seat she hoped to defend at the next election and the Diary speculated that the 24-year-old Cameron would move to Downing Street from the Conservative research department. In fact, he lost out to Jonathan Hill, who 20 years later became Cameron's leader in the House of Lords and an EU commissioner.

Sometimes a debut appearance gives no hint of what is to come. Margaret Thatcher first appeared in 1966, but in a fairly low-key story about the opposition to Labour's selective employment tax. The Queen was also there from the beginning, although again it was an inauspicious introduction: an item on the guests attending a service for Commonwealth Day. A ferret through the archive finds early mentions for some of our acting royalty, too, such as Ian McKellen, in an item in 1970 about his Hamlet, or Judi Dench, when she was appearing in *A Midsummer Night's Dream* in 1967.

11

The Times Diary, unlike say the *Evening Standard's* diary, has always steered clear of "society" photographs of the famous and beautiful drinking champagne at parties. Instead, at various points of its history, it has reflected the more playful nature of the column by the use of pocket cartoons, drawn by the likes of Barry Fantoni, Jonathan Pugh, Neil Bennett, David Haldane and Geoff Thompson. Some of them, particularly Fantoni, based their cartoons on news stories, while others were free to draw on any subject. We've selected a few to illustrate the chapters of this anthology.

The Diary has occasionally got into trouble with the authorities. In 1985, a leak inquiry was launched in the Commons to find who had passed PHS the details of the draft of a select committee report on the Special Branch. Twenty MPs gave evidence that it was not them. Claire Short, who would become Tony Blair's international development secretary, said: "If I am going to leak anything I would not leak it to a disreputable paper like *The Times*." The committee of privileges met late at night to discuss the issue. A report of that session was also leaked to PHS.

The column also received a complaint in the mid-1990s from Margaret Thatcher after a story that Anthony-Noel Kelly, a sculptor jailed for stealing body parts from the Royal College of Surgeons, had fashioned a pair of door handles from human bones for Carol Thatcher, the former prime minister's daughter. Our reporter had talked his way into Thatcher's flat to investigate, but it turned out that the handles had been made from bone casts and apologies and retractions duly followed.

The Diary also sparked a diplomatic incident in 2000 when the Belgian ambassador to London told a reporter at a party that his new prime minister had offered Tony Blair the use of his Tuscan villa for a holiday. Downing Street went ballistic, Alastair Campbell, Blair's spin doctor, demanded that the reporter be sacked (he's now on the *Mail on Sunday*) and the ambassador retracted his story. He may now have been posted to the Falklands. Those last two spats occurred when the Diary editor was Jasper Gerard, now chief press officer for the Liberal Democrats, proof that there is no end to how far a Diary editor can go.

The Diary corner of the office was long seen as a bit of a children's playground. Gerard and his team, finding a blank wall next to them, used to play squash against it. When I joined the Diary team as a junior reporter under the editorship of Giles Coren, son of Alan, in 2001, there was a dartboard on the wall. Colleagues had to look both ways before crossing in front of our desks.

Coren's Diary was seldom concerned with stories in the traditional sense. He was keen on parlour games and long-running series, such as inviting readers to send in their favourite jokes in German (believing there is no such thing as German humour) or, feeling that we only see the word manger at Christmas, attempting to use it in his column once a week for a year. When one reader, Reg Tripp, wrote to complain about Coren, he was invited to join the Diary team and gamely came along for a couple of days. In September of that year, though, the Diary was felt to be too frivolous for the serious times the world faced after 9/11 and the column was moved from the comment pages to the Times2 features supplement for a couple of months.

Near the end of 2001, Coren became the paper's restaurant critic, thus getting him out of the last two months of his "manger" pledge, and Jack Malvern became Diary editor. A year later, the Diary column was moved from the comment page and reborn as People on the news pages, initially written by Andrew Pierce, then Hugo Rifkind and Adam Sherwin. It showed how the boundary between Diary stories and proper news had become blurred since 1966. Some important personality-based stories were broken in the Diary, such as Rifkind disclosing that

Tony Blair planned to convert to Catholicism, but it still retained some silliness. By 2009, though, with the world again a serious place after the global financial crash, the Diary was culled.

"One day the world will be a happy, rich, flippant place again and the Diary will be back," Rifkind said at the time. This happened in 2013 when John Witherow, the Editor of *The Times*, asked me to resuscitate the column. Flippancy and silliness were encouraged. In our first discussion about it we agreed that we would never just do stories about posh girls in pretty frocks at garden parties. Political gossip played a big role, but we were interested in anything that made us laugh or perplexed.

Some stories were "followed" by other newspapers, who even put some of them on their front page (such as the one about Ed Miliband, then the leader of the Labour party and hoping to become prime minister, being voted the fourth most influential person in Doncaster; or the news that "Boaty McBoatface" was the early leader in a poll to name a new scientific research vessel), but breaking news was always a low priority compared to providing an antidote to the news.

The latest reboot of the Diary was called TMS, which not only suggests the word *Times* if you omit the vowels but referred to our then office in Thomas More Square and was thus a nod back to the old days of PHS. We kept the title of TMS even after moving into new offices in London Bridge Street. After all, PHS had lasted until 1988, even though *The Times* had moved by that time from Printing House Square to Grey's Inn Road and then Pennington Street.

TMS to many will always suggest *Test Match Special*, the BBC's cricket commentary, and to some extent there is a connection. Brian Johnston, the great cricket commentator, once said that his vision of TMS was a gathering of old friends at a cricket match who chat away about anything and everything as well as the action in front of them. If anyone had a good joke or story, they would share it with their listeners, as anyone watching the cricket from the stands would do. This chimed with my own vision of what the Diary should be, a gathering of jokes and stories for the amusement of friends, those being our readers.

Stories come from all over the place, including in the traditional way of buying indiscreet MPs enough drink until they say something amusing. There is a small network of freelance Diary hounds who forage through magazines and local newspapers looking for snippets that will earn them a tip fee. Colleagues whose day job is writing serious journalism will pass me the lighter items that they can't get into the paper in exchange for a bottle of gin. I like to encourage also readers to send in amusing things that they have spotted, for which they get their name plugged in the column.

And then there are the Diary elves, the twentysomethings starting out in journalism, who we send out to parties and events with a mission to speak to enough people until they can come back with a story. "I don't miss that at all," Rifkind says. "Celebrities either ignore you, which is humiliating, or are desperate to speak to you, which is embarrassing." Like all sensible Diary editors, he selected only the plum events to attend himself. I have always preferred to get stories over a long lunch with one source than in a packed room. Nonetheless, without the dedication and desperation of our elves, the column would never get filled.

This anthology gives a flavour of what the *Times* Diary has been about for half a century. There are plenty of famous names – politicians, actors, royalty – but also stories included simply because they made us laugh at the time. In dark times, laughter is the best medicine. I hope you enjoy it.

Patrick Kidd, *Times* Diary editor, July 2016

ACKNOWLEDGMENTS

I owe great thanks to Kaya Burgess, my deputy since 2013, for his friendship and support and Grant Tucker, also known as the Diary hobbit, the best networker in town. The column would never get filled without the industry of our freelance reporters and tipsters and the cast-offs off my colleagues – too many to list but you know who you are and have drunk the profits.

This book would never have been compiled without the many hours spent burrowing in the archives by Holly Smith and without the patience and encouragement of Jethro Lennox and Sarah Woods at HarperCollins. Thank you also to John Witherow and Emma Tucker, Editor and Deputy Editor of *The Times*, and to whoever suggested to them that the person to bring back the Diary should be the newspaper's rowing correspondent, as I was at the time. And thank you to all our readers, especially those who send in their own offerings.

Above all, thank you to Ruth and Hattie, my wife and daughter, for tolerating my absences in the evenings and for being the sounding board for so many bad puns.

COURT IN
THE ACT

In that brief heatwave we had a month ago, legal minds became a little frazzled. A barrister tells me that he heard his opposing counsel ask a court official to give the air conditioning a boost. "It's controlled by the knob on the bench," the clerk explained. The QC, assuming this to be a lack of deference rather than a reference to a dial, addressed the judge: "M'Lud, I'm told that you control the air conditioning." (2015)

. . .

The QC who thought the "knob on the bench" referred to the judge rather than the heating dial has brought more stories of courtroom faux pas. One reader recalls, in the days before email, a judge who realised he'd left a key document at home. "Fax it up, m'lud?" suggested one of the barristers. "Yes, it does rather," replied the judge. (2015)

. . .

Today's entry for my jurisprudery series on filthy mishearings in court comes from Fran Burgess, who tells of a judge who got increasingly annoyed at the defendant chewing gum. "Instruct that man to cease masticating," he told the clerk, at which the official, red-faced, turned to the defendant and said: "Oi. Take your hands out of your pockets." (2015)

. . .

The combination of my series on jurisprudery and yesterday's item about Evelyn Waugh led John Gregory to forward an entry from Waugh's diaries. It featured a judge who was trying a sodomy case and, uncertain about the guidelines for sentencing, went to consult Lord Birkenhead, the lord chancellor. "What should you give a man who allows himself to be buggered?" the judge asked, to which the peer absentmindedly replied: "Oh, 30 shillings or two pounds, whatever you happen to have on you." (2015)

. . .

William Rees-Davies, controversial barrister and Tory MP for Thanet West, is the subject of one of the longer-lasting, though probably apocryphal, legal jokes. Appearing for a defendant on a criminal charge, he was in full flow with a lengthy speech in mitigation, of which his client showed increasing signs of disapproval, eventually scribbling a note to his counsel. The judge noticed and asked what it was about. "Nothing, M'Lud, merely a billet-doux from my client," replied Rees-Davies. "It seems to me, judging by his behaviour in the dock," riposted the judge, "that it is rather more in the line of a Billy Don't." (1980)

. . .

Ernie Money, Conservative MP for Ipswich, tells me that his father and Lord Goddard, the former lord chief justice who died on Saturday, were contemporaries at Marlborough. As new boys, they were expected to undergo a "dormitory test", such as reciting a poem or singing a song. When it came to his turn, Goddard, at 13, astounded his school-fellows by reciting the death sentence. (1971)

. . .

Court No 1 at the Old Bailey was packed yesterday for a valedictory tribute to Judge Brian Barker on his retirement as Recorder of London, or senior nibs at the Central Criminal Court. Sir Brian Leveson revealed that Barker had failed his Latin GCE three times but still liked to boast of his knowledge of Roman culture. On one occasion his junior clerk was grappling with a crossword. "Dog star, six letters," the lackey said. "That's easy," Barker replied. "It's Sirius." The next morning his clerk complained about being misled. The correct answer should have been "Lassie". (2015)

• • •

Jeremy Hutchinson, the celebrated lawyer who turns 101 next week, spoke the other night about some of his most famous cases. He was once defending a case of alleged buggery, he said, and the prosecution made a damning remark against his client. The judge turned to Hutchinson and said: "Well, there's a shot across the bows." Quick as a flash, Hutchinson replied: "More a shot across the stern, I would have thought." (2016)

• • •

A quick legal story from Dai George, a solicitor who was acting in a divorce case where the wife alleged that her husband was a drunk. "Have you discussed going to Alcoholics Anonymous with your doctor?" the judge asked, to which the man replied: "I didn't know my doctor went to Alcoholics Anonymous." (2015)

• • •

The brand new headquarters of the law firm Eversheds opens in Manchester this month and to celebrate the big event the company held an internal competition to give the new building a name. According to an Eversheds brochure I have in front of me, "entries ranged from the quite good to the rather strange". After much deliberation those wacky fellows plumped for "Eversheds House." Makes you wonder what the "quite good" suggestions were. (2001)

Irvine Smith, a Scottish sheriff known for his turn of phrase, once presided over a trial of two homosexuals, when it was still a crime. Noting their distress, Smith caused giggles in court by declaring: "I'm going to defer sentence to give you time to pull yourselves together." (2015)

. . .

London stipendiary magistrate Eric Crowther writes in the current issue of the Magistrates' Association magazine of a woman convicted for soliciting who asked for time to pay her fine. "How long do you need?" asked the bench. "About 20 minutes should do", she replied. (1986)

. . .

Today's legal story involves an indecency trial at which a witness was too embarrassed to say out loud what the defendant was alleged to have said to her. The judge suggested that she write it down and the note was passed round the court. The final man in the jury box had nodded off, however, so the woman next to him had to give a nudge before passing him the paper. He read it, blinked, turned to her and whispered: "What? Here?" (2015)

. . .

Skulking around the gents toilets at the Law Courts recently, a reader overheard two judges having a giggle. Apparently they had just been to lunch with a prominent firm of solicitors before which this adapted Grace was said: "For those whom we are about to deceive, may the Lord make our clients truly thankful." (2014)

Dozens of cafeterias at crown courts are being closed after the contract with Eurest ended last month. Chris Grayling, the justice secretary, has decided to halt the government subsidy of catering contracts, meaning that judges, jurors, defendants and witnesses will all have to venture out for a sarnie at lunchtime. It may be a wise idea. The advocates' mess at Snaresbrook has been closed for ages after human urine was found in food. Best not to order the pee soup. (2014)

"There's Frost on the lawn."

FILM AND
TELEVISION

Jonathan Ross spoke fondly on Tuesday of his friendship with Sir Michael Caine, who told him about the smoke-filled evenings he had spent with Noël Coward while filming *The Italian Job*. On one occasion, Coward arrived looking ill. "I've got a dreadful pain in my backside, Michael," he said. "And the doctor couldn't find anything wrong." After much prodding, the doctor asked him exactly where he was feeling pain. "Near the entrance," Coward told him. At this, the doctor looked up. "In my line of work," he said. "We prefer to refer to it as an exit." (2015)

. . .

Party managers have just been confronted with a terrible new dilemma. In a year or two the party conferences are to be televised in colour, and a trial run of the Conservative party conference in Brighton during October produced horrifying pictures. There were red carpets in the conference hall and red chair covers and the decor included large Union flags. As a consequence, Mr Heath and all his front-bench team, not to say the rank-and-file constituency representatives, come out on the BBC colour film looking like boiled lobsters. The redness of the decor had become all-pervasive. One Conservative party manager said yesterday that no time would be lost in solving the problem. But how? Will the political parties have to foot the bill for the hire of new carpets and chair covers? And will a Conservative conference be the same without a plentiful showing of Union flags. As the party manager said: "We shall have to get in somebody who knows about these things to advise us." It looks like the birth of a new perquisite for out-of-work stage designers and lighting technicians. (1967)

A tale was told by Lord Puttnam at yesterday's memorial service for Richard Attenborough about a rather awkward press conference he held on the release of *Gandhi* in Delhi. No one wanted to ask the first question until a woman raised her hand. "Why did you make this?" she said. "Gandhi is a deity to us. By showing him in a loincloth, you can only diminish him." Attenborough sweetly asked how she would have done it. "I'd have shown him as a moving ball of light that illuminates our lives," she said, to which Attenborough replied: "I wasn't making a film about bloody Tinkerbell." (2015)

• • •

It seems Martin Scorsese would stop at nothing to get Cate Blanchett to play Katharine Hepburn in *The Aviator*, his Howard Hughes biopic. "For the part of Hepburn, get me the girl who was in *Elizabeth*," he told his casting director. "If you can't get her, get me the girl in *Veronica Guerin*. If you can't get her, get me the girl in *The Shipping News*." The Australian played all three roles. (2004)

• • •

Norman Giller, a veteran hack-of-all-trades, has just published his autobiography. He spent 14 years as a writer on *This Is Your Life* and recalls flying to Los Angeles with the host, Eamonn Andrews, to ambush the British actor Dudley Moore. In the green room, one Hollywood starlet sighed: "God, I could do with some coke." Eager to oblige, Andrews went to the bar and brought back a Coca-Cola. "Not that kind of coke," she told him, looking as if he was mad. So Andrews returned to the bar and got her a Pepsi. (2015)

Writing and starring in hit series such as *The League of Gentlemen* and *Sherlock* has made Mark Gatiss a household face, but not yet a household name, he admits. Speaking at a London Lesbian and Gay Switchboard event, Gatiss recalled checking into a Cardiff hotel late one night to be accosted by the awe-struck porter. "Oh Christ almighty. This is amazing," the porter said. "I've got to ring my wife about this. I can't believe I've met ... what's your name again?" (2014)

• • •

Delivering the Hugh Cudlipp Memorial Lecture last night, Alastair Campbell, the former Downing Street spin doctor, listed the TV offers that came his way when he left No 10. "I could have been a celebrity dog trainer, a celebrity safari game warden, a celebrity cabbie, a celebrity circus performer, a celebrity shark diver, a celebrity nurse, a celebrity teacher, a judge in a celebrity chef contest, a celebrity conductor – of orchestras not buses," he said.

"My favourite," Campbell added, "was the one asking me to have medical treatment to turn me into a black man then make a film exposing racism in the Deep South. "Intrigued, I asked if all of me went black. 'I think so,' came the reply. 'And can I go back to being white at a time of my choosing?' I asked. 'I'll have to check but I think so'." (2008)

Meryl Streep's latest film is an adaptation of *Into the Woods*, the Stephen Sondheim musical based on the Grimm fairytales. When she was being considered for the part of the witch, Streep was summoned before Sondheim, who told her to belt out a few of the songs. At the end of the audition she asked if she could keep the sheet music. "Of course," he replied. And would he autograph it? "By all means." It was only later, she said at the film's London launch yesterday, that she looked at what he had written. It said: "Don't f••• it up." (2015)

• • •

He cannot get the bums on seats. Lord Puttnam, the film producer, had an awkward time addressing the Tiverton Labour Society. "There was only one person in the audience but he applauded wildly and made up for the lack of numbers. When I finished my talk I said: 'There isn't much point in having a question and answer session, so I think I'll pack up and catch my train'." His listener registered grave disappointment and said he would greatly appreciate my staying. "When I asked him why my presence was so important, he replied: 'I'm the next speaker'." (1998)

• • •

Lecherous film producers have always abounded in Hollywood and Sir Roger Moore tells a good story about one in his new memoir, *Last Man Standing*. It concerns Darryl F Zanuck, the priapic former boss of 20th Century Fox, who had a thing about Joans, trying and failing to bed Crawford and Collins. Zanuck kept a solid-gold, life-size mould of his manhood on his desk and once showed it off to Crawford. "Impressive, huh?" he said. She replied witheringly: "I've seen bigger things crawl out of cabbages." (2014)

In *Baywatch*, the 1990s TV series about lifeguards, the women spent most of their time running on the beach, very slowly, in tight outfits. This was not just to please sofa perverts. In a talk at the London Apple store, David Hasselhoff, who played the male lead, said it was also for budgetary reasons: "We had no money and were eight minutes short [on the pilot], so we shot everybody in slow-motion." It gave their ratings an extra bounce. (2014)

. . .

The National TV Licence Records office is commendably thorough in its checks on the use of unlicensed television sets. They have just sent one of their inquiry forms addressed to: "The Present Occupier, Harwich Town Mortuary". (1976)

. . .

Playing Stephen Hawking in *The Theory of Everything*, a biopic of the cosmologist's first marriage, was a tall order for Eddie Redmayne, who said studying black holes was tough for a history of art graduate who "gave up science at 14". Promoting the film has been equally tricky, he said at a *Wired* magazine Q&A with Professor Hawking. "When I did *Les Misérables*, every interview would end with someone saying: 'Will you sing something?' That was pretty horrific and I would say: 'No, no, no.' I thought this film would be much easier and it was, until people started asking if I could explain the intricacies of $E=mc^2$. I had to say: 'God, no. But I can sing for you?'" (2014)

Stephen Merchant, the co-creator of *The Office*, is hoping to crack America with a starring role in an HBO sitcom called *Hello Ladies* that starts next week. Merchant has long complained about his luck in love, and fame has not made the search for romance any easier. "What happens is that your aspirations change," he says. "Now I get rejected by much more beautiful women." (2013)

• • •

An appropriate challenger has been found to take on the wordy television personality Nicholas Parsons in an attempt on his world after-dinner speaking record of 428 minutes 3 seconds. He is the similarly prolific author and broadcaster Gyles Brandreth who held the previous record.

Already the insults have begun to fly from Mr Brandreth who established his reputation as a talker in 1969. Then, as a 21-year-old student, he appeared on television and talked Fred Friendly, the American commentator, Lady Longford, Ian MacLeod and Michael Foot off the screen in a 90-minute confrontation. Mr Brandreth said: "Of course, Nicholas is used to performing in front of an audience that's fast asleep so he has an advantage over me there." (1978)

• • •

So risibly horrific do American audiences find Michael Winner's *Death Trap*, I am told, that as the moment approaches when Michael Caine and Christopher Reeves kiss each other the customers at Loew's cinema on Broadway rise in their seats and yell: "Don't do it, Superman."[1] (1982)

---

[1]   Reeve appeared as Superman in the 1978 film.

A personal obituary of Lauren Bacall, the American actress, star of *The Big Sleep*, which was paid for by Leonard Bernstein's children, appeared in yesterday's *New York Times*. "We are sad to have lost a long-time friend," the composer's offspring wrote. "[Her] appearance at the back door of the Bernstein apartment at the Dakota was always a welcome delight — even if she was complaining about the piano noise." (2014)

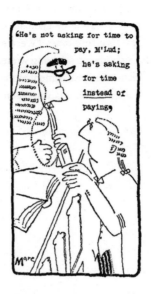

CRIME AND PUNISHMENT

The Metropolitan police calls time for the last time tonight at its much-loved headquarters' watering-hole: "The Tank". Situated on the ground floor of New Scotland Yard, the windowless bar has been a favourite since the building opened in the 1960s. In keeping with new commissioner Paul Condon's stated aim of making the Met more "user-friendly", the tank will be closed and replaced by a gym. According to one Scotland Yard insider, "The powers-that-be thought that the smell of beery fumes in reception did nothing for our public image." Will the sight of gasping, red-faced, overweight detectives be an improvement? Or, indeed, be very different? (1993)

• • •

I was burgled last weekend and have been thinking about how to improve security. I am wondering whether to take a leaf out of the book of Labour MP Chris Mullin, whose flat in Brixton Road was burgled seven times in two years. Eventually, to avoid continually replacing broken locks and smashed doors, he took to pinning a note on his door saying: "Dear burglar, the door is unlocked. I have now been robbed so many times that if you can find anything of value remaining you are welcome to it. Please close the door again on your way out." (1990)

• • •

Jonathan Aitken, the former cabinet minister, gave a speech on prison reform yesterday and recalled his first day behind bars after being convicted of perjury in 1999. He was seen by the prison psychiatrist, who was unaware of his famous patient and asked for assorted personal information. Then he said: "Does anyone other than your family know you are in prison?" Aitken smiled. "About 20 million people," he said. The psychiatrist was taken aback and looked over his glasses at the patient. "Have you ever suffered from delusions?" he asked. (2016)

Central TV was delighted when its film crew was called out to report a successful victim-support scheme in Preston. Proud policemen led them to the home of an elderly woman who had been burgled but was now an exemplary pupil of their lessons on home security. Unfortunately, she had learnt too well: despite every blandishment shouted through the letter-box, she refused to open up. "The police have told me not to," she said sternly. (1986)

• • •

It looks as if a Neighbourhood Watch scheme in Chiswick, west London, has a few things to learn about crime prevention. Organisers have just popped a circular through doors inviting every householder in two streets on a "get to know you" day trip to Boulogne on a specified Saturday next month. Should give the criminal fraternity a clear run. (1987)

• • •

Boris Johnson was posed a riddle yesterday in his last London mayor's question time. If the crime rate has fallen, why don't police have more time to solve fewer remaining crimes? Deploying trademark Borisian logic, Johnson suggested it must be because police have already caught all the rubbish criminals. "I think it's possible that when you have huge falls in something like burglary," he said, "the remaining burglars that you have operational are likely to be the ones that are difficult to catch." (2016)

After making an impassioned speech for more bobbies on the beat, Martin Thomas, SDP candidate for Wrexham, left the HTV studio to discover that his car had been stolen, along with a batch of party literature on crime prevention. (1987)

• • •

There is more to the innocent antiques advert at the back of this month's *Country Life* than meets the eye: "Wilfred Bull, dealer in antiques ... wishes to buy walnut or mahogany furniture for a handsome price and would welcome any invitation to call and see you." In 15 years' time, perhaps. The millionaire dealer from Coggeshall in Essex has a permanent booking for the ad and failed to cancel it when given a life sentence for murdering his wife. (1986)

• • •

Dominic Kennedy, our investigations editor, received a letter last week from a loyal fan who is doing a long stretch at HMP Frankland after being convicted of murder. "Dear Mr Kennedy," it began. "Hope you had a good Christmas and new year. Mine? I decided to stay in ..." (2014)

• • •

Action stations at a North Yorkshire police station. A drowsy-voiced telephone caller warns of a plan to dump a body in the boating lake of a nearby amusement park. The duty sergeant presses for more information, but the caller has passed out. In the background, however, the plotters can faintly be heard, scheming away. The call is traced. Police cars race to the address. The officers burst into the house ... and find a rather confused but public-spirited old man, the phone still in his hand. He had been watching a melodramatic edition of *Hi-de-Hi!*[2] (1986)

---

[2]   *Hi-de-Hi!* was a British situation comedy set in a holiday camp in the early 1960s

When the debate turns to law and order, the shadow home secretary, Jack Straw, should look to his leader for tips. A report has emerged in New York of how Tony Blair was locked up in prison four years ago in the Big Apple. He was doing Straw's job, on a fact-finding mission, visiting the Metropolitan Correctional Centre at the time. Being shown round by a prison official, he was in an empty section at the top of the high-rise prison when a door clanged shut behind him. "Don't worry, there's a phone in here," the prison official reassured them. The phone didn't work, and Blair and his party were locked in for four hours until rescued by another screw. (1997)

• • •

Masterly British understatement? Mrs Maggie Blackhouse has just divorced her husband, Graham, who is serving a prison sentence for murdering a neighbour and trying to blow her up with a car bomb. Her grounds: unreasonable behaviour. (1986)

• • •

The actors Martin and Gary Kemp attended a 25th-anniversary screening of their film *The Krays* at the BFI and spoke of being allowed to interview Ronnie Kray at Broadmoor. The gangster clearly had the place under his thumb. After their chat in the hospital cafe, Gary Kemp was given the bill and protested that £100 seemed rather steep for two non-alcoholic lagers. "Ronnie put a few fags on the bill," the server, another inmate, explained, then added with very polite malice: "I hope you don't mind." Kemp decided that it was wise to pay up. (2015)

Stan Turner, stage-doorman at the Royal Opera House, Covent Garden, was confronted by a uniformed police sergeant from the Bow Street station just round the corner. "I have reason to believe", said the law, "that you can help me with my enquiries." Turner blanched. "Me and the other blokes in the nick are doing a crossword", the sergeant continued, "and we want to know Mozart's first name." (1973)

*"You're the fifth Ringo we've
had . . ."*

APT NAMES

A recurring series in the Diary in recent years has featured people with appropriate names for their jobs, or what an article in 1994 in *New Scientist* magazine called "nominative determinism". Their examples included an expert on subterranean London called Trench and the urologists Splatt and Weedon. A few years later, I had been amused to see two experts summoned to give evidence to the Commons health committee on the obesity crisis. Their names were Crisp and Podger.

In fact, the Times Diary had been playing this game 20 years before *New Scientist* gave it a title. In 1974, PHS had noted a few well-named individuals, such as Inspector Barker, head of the dogs section of Merseyside Police, and Mrs Serff, of the department of medieval history at University College, Dublin.

Inspired by the retirement of Lord Judge as Lord Chief Justice in 2013 (and the fact that there was an Inspector Crook at my local police station), I invited readers to send in more examples of apt names that they had spotted. So far we have received more than 400 entries.

There was the Aberdeen golf professional called Donald Slicer; the department for education's chief schools adjudicator, Elizabeth Passmore; and the former surveyor of the fabric of Westminster Abbey, Donald Buttress. Then there was Lisa Falco, a handler at the Imperial Bird of Prey Academy; Robin Banks of Bedfordshire Police (surely a name that belongs more to those he catches) and an associate in social work called Mr Burden.

We also had some entries from overseas, such as the South African funeral services company called Human and Pitt, and a vet near Dunkirk by the name of Nathalie Miaux. She must specialise in cats.

On a medical theme, we had a midwife called Tugwell and another called Stork, an orthopaedic surgeon called Breakwell, a urologist called Waterfall, a paediatric nurse called Smallbones and a surgeon who did hip replacements called Hopgood. Among the dentists brought to my attention were ones with the names Nashar, Fang and Fillingham. And there was a dentist in Folkestone called George Au. Presumably he specialised in gold fillings.

The church was also a good place to find apt names. There was the churchwarden called Proverbs, the organists at York Minster called Sharpe and Pipe and the ecclesiastically complete Canon Bishop, vicar of Deane.

Quite a few readers suggested the Sligo solicitors Argue & Phibbs. Wright Hassall, a law firm in Leamington Spa, is also perfectly named, as is the Kidderminster estate agent Doolittle and Dalley. We also had a reader who went to university with a man called Lawless. He became a solicitor and married a girl called Swindells. The best man was Cheetham.

One reader recalled his days working for Thames Conservancy. "My boss was Mr Banks and his assistant Mr Lock," he wrote. "The chief purification officer was Mr Fish, whose secretary was Miss Poole." Another wrote to complain that "for reasons of credibility it is many years since I gained a break in a holiday competition". His name: Bill Wintrip

Then there was the case of the man accused of masturbating under Boscombe Pier. The arresting officer, of course, was PC Fiddler. And the story from Canada about a man who was charged after being caught exposing his genitals in a park. His name: Donald Popadick.

And who can forget the campaign director of Stonewall, the gay rights organisation: Mr Twococock. Pull the other one, I said, but it was true. Lucky Mr Twococock.

THE POWER
AND THE TORY

Boris Johnson tells a good story in his new biography of Churchill of when the PM was told that a minister had been caught in a compromising position one February morning. "Did I hear you correctly that so-and-so has been caught with a Guardsman?" he asked his chief whip. "In Hyde Park? On a park bench? At three o'clock in the morning?" The chief whip answered in the affirmative to all. Churchill puffed on his cigar. "In this weather?" he added. "Good God, man. It makes you proud to be British." (2014)

• • •

A news item about a Conservative politician who mistakenly canvassed the wife of the Labour MP in the neighbouring constituency reminded John Disley, a reader, of a story told at the memorial service of James Allason, the Tory MP and architect of the right-to-buy policy. Allason was sent to campaign in a strongly working-class constituency and at one house the door was opened by a man wearing a string vest. Allason introduced himself politely, then apologised for "interrupting a chap while he was dressing for dinner". (2015)

• • •

Enoch Powell's feud with Sir Edward Heath and politicians of his ilk is expected to continue posthumously. Before his death yesterday, Powell, who was sacked from the shadow cabinet by Heath after his infamous "Rivers of Blood" speech on immigration in 1968 had cooperated extensively with Simon Heffer, the right-wing commentator, on an authorised biography detailing his life and foes.

His help, however, was on condition that the book remained unpublished during his lifetime. Now Powell is dead, we can all look forward to some excoriating critiques from beyond the grave. But whatever one thinks about Powell's more colourful views, his intellect seemed to terrify even his wife. Margaret Powell said: "After the first year of our marriage, I felt I had received a university education." (1998)

. . .

For the first time a woman has been invited to deliver the annual Tory Party conference lecture staged by the Conservative Political Centre, an opportunity much coveted by the party's intellectuals through the years – and certainly the best chance a high-flying Tory politician ever gets to influence party thinking on a major theme. The choice has fallen on Mrs Margaret Thatcher, formerly a taxation specialist and now in the shadow cabinet as lead voice on Power. She has chosen as her theme "What's wrong with politics?". Daughter of a Grantham grocer who became a golden-voiced local alderman, Mrs Thatcher used a brilliant Oxford career to make herself an industrial chemist, married and switched to the Bar, then switched again to where she really wanted to be: Westminster. She is a blonde bluestocking of peat charm, and not only Tories in the House think she has a better brain, if less demagogic skill, than Barbara Castle, to whom she is the Tory Party's answer.[3] (1968)

. . .

Labour has its pink minivan and the Greens have a double-decker run on vegetable oil but no one does a literal "battle bus" like Margaret Thatcher did. An armoured 36-seater that was built for Mrs Thatcher and her cabinet to use after the Brighton bombing in 1984 has been

---

[3]   While Mrs Thatcher had first appeared in the Diary in 1966, this was the first detailed discussion of her talents.

43

put up for sale by a company called Tanks a Lot. The vehicle has bullet-proof glass, an extra-thick anti-blast floor and run-flat tyres, as well as a couple of bullet holes in the side, which may be from when the army used it in Ulster.

The asking price of £25,000 is the same as one of Mrs Thatcher's handbags sold for at auction in 2011 and the seller, Nick Mead, hopes that it might attract an American collector of Maggie memorabilia. "I found a blue umbrella under the back seat that could have been hers," Mead, a shrewd salesman, says. "And a pair of knickers, although they seem too skimpy to be Maggie's. Maybe they belonged to Edwina Currie?"[4] (2015)

• • •

It was my daughter's fourth birthday party on Sunday. When I mentioned this in passing to Baroness Jenkin of Kennington, she recalled taking her son to parliament at the same age, when her MP husband, Bernard, was a Maastricht rebel. "I'm FOUR," the boy declared in the canteen. "That's good," said his grandfather, a former cabinet minister. "Your father is generally against." (2014)

• • •

It could have all been so different. Nina Bawden, the novelist, who was at Oxford with Margaret Thatcher, remembers confronting her over joining the Tory party. "I told her it was disgraceful, particularly as she was a grammar school girl like me," she says in *New Statesman*. "She defended herself by saying that Conservatives were so dull she would have more chance of getting into parliament." (2005)

---

[4] Edwina Currie, a former junior health minister, confessed in 2002 to a four-year affair with John Major before he became prime minister.

Jacob Rees-Mogg[5] may seem like the MP for Fusty-upon-Tweed, but beware the sharp tongue lurking within the double-breasted suit. In a *Question Time* debate on building a third runway at Heathrow, Rees-Mogg declared: "I used to live not a million miles from Slough, with the aeroplanes going over, and I must confess they didn't prove too bothersome then." Sensing some creative understatement, David Dimbleby cast him a wry glance and asked: "Eton, was that?" The audience laughed, before Mogg, with perfect comic timing and a withering tone, turned to a rather smug Dimbleby and noted: "I was at school with your son." (2015)

· · ·

Congratulations to Stephen Crabb[6] on becoming a pub quiz answer. The new Welsh secretary is the first Tory cabinet minister to have a beard since the Earl of Onslow in 1905. The Tories have never been comfortable with hirsuteness — Thatcher, on making Nigel Lawson chancellor, told him to cut his hair before doing the same to the budget — and especially not beards. Ernest Marples, John Gummer and Greg Knight were all told to shave if they wanted to get ahead. David Blunkett once suggested a reason why there are so few beards on the right: "Tory MPs have more time on their hands to shave." (2014)

· · ·

In *The Lady's Not For Spurning*, to be shown on BBC Four on Monday, Michael Portillo looks at the legacy of Baroness Thatcher. Highlights include his recollection of sitting in the Commons and seeing Thatcher heading, for the first time, to the back benches. "How do you think the

---

[5] Son of a former *Times* editor. MP for North East Somerset since 2010. A Diary favourite.

[6] Who stood for the leadership of the Conservative party in 2016.

prime minister is coping?" whispered John Major, leaning in. "She's not the prime minister," Portillo reminded him. "You are." (2008)

• • •

George Osborne, the proud and profligate wooer of Becky Sharp in *Vanity Fair*, may be the most famous fictional namesake in politics, but the *London Review of Books* has unearthed another in a 1967 science fiction novel. In *Agent of Chaos* by Norman Spinrad, a writer on the original *Star Trek*, Boris Johnson is the bumbling leader of an inter-planetary resistance movement fighting a totalitarian regime. "Boris Johnson was quite willing to babble on — and did so at every opportunity," Spinrad wrote, prophetically. Perhaps a video of the mayor of London's speeches found its way back to the 1960s through a rift in the space-time continuum? "I've been aware of the 'real' Boris for years," Spinrad tells me. "Sometimes I wonder if he read the novel and couldn't help but pattern his political stance after the fictional one." (2014)

• • •

Spotted in *Time* magazine, Boris Johnson was asked whether he considers himself to be a conviction politician. "I certainly have a range of convictions," he declares. "Not for anything serious. God. I don't have convictions, actually, by the way. No, no, no. Sorry, I don't have any convictions in a court of law, apart from speeding when I was very young. But I have plenty of political convictions. Can you rescue me?" Later Boris declares his wish no longer to be seen as "bumbling". Best of luck with that. (2008)

When does a has-been become a bigwig? When you can kick today's government by using the sins of forgotten men. Thus, despite being out of frontline politics since 1997, David Mellor was called a "Tory grandee" in yesterday's *Sun* after being pompous towards a cabbie[7]. It gives an excuse for a Mellor story, told to me by one of his former comrades. When news broke in 1992 of Mellor's affair with the actress Antonia de Sancha, one ruddy-faced knight of the shires was seen shaking with rage in the Commons tea room, brandishing a paper that had a photo of the love nest. "What a disgrace," Bufton-Tufton thundered. "It's only a shag," another MP protested. "I don't care about that, look at this," the knight said, pointing to a bottle by the lovers' mattress. "Cypriot sherry! What is this party coming to?" (2014)

• • •

At the launch of the Bow Group's Conservative Revival this week, a speaker remarked of George Osborne's career that "the only thing that rises faster is Boris Johnson on Viagra!" Osborne kept a straight face. A fellow Tory Alan Duncan, also present, didn't. (2006)

• • •

Jacob Rees-Mogg is an admirably old-school politician who believes in the virtue of meeting the electorate face to face, albeit with his nanny and chauffeur close at hand. In an interview with Mogg on the Conservative Home website, a story is told about when he was seeking election in Fife in 1997 and arrived at a hall for a public meeting to find only one woman and a small child present. Moggster's agent suggested it wasn't worth bothering with, but the candidate insisted and proceeded to address this woman as if he were Gladstone for

---

7   In fact, he rose no higher than secretary of state for national heritage.

half an hour. Eventually she raised her hand. "Excuse me," she asked politely. "Is the mother and toddler group cancelled?" (2014)

. . .

If the bumblings of Boris Johnson are merely a pose, then they are a pose with a long pedigree. Extracted from the University of Oxford's *Cherwell* newspaper, dated November 2, 1984: "Canine Boris Johnson is clearly taking a leaf out of Ronald Reagan's campaign book. The shaggy and outwardly incompetent Union secretary now has freshers on their knees screaming 'four more terms' – and all a result of his endearing pretence of approaching senility. Fluffing his speeches and breaking the Union's tape recorder last week were clearly just a deliberate attempt to win sympathy and votes. The hangdog has realised that in the Union, as in American politics, if you convince the punters that you're stupider than they, you cannot go wrong." We shall see. (2007)

. . .

"I was in a shop on Highbury Corner," e-mails a reader. "An odd-looking fellow came rushing in, asked for some eggs and told the owner that he would be back in five minutes to pay for them. I followed him out, and saw Boris Johnson crossing the street. Egg-man started throwing. Boris started effing and blinding and tried to push the man away in a rather girly way with his knees. Then a black cab turned up. Boris got in, but then decided to get out again to hurl some abuse. In all the excitement, he fell over. You might be able to use this in your column." (2006)

A very early wake-up call from Boris Johnson, after our revelation that he was targeted by an egg-wielding yob in darkest Islington. "The important point is this," says Boris, "the tosser missed. I am a corpulent Conservative shadow minister. Not a small target. Yet not one drop of albumen spattered my suit! A terrible indictment of the sporting ability of today's youth. I blame the Government. No wonder we lost so badly to Bangladesh. Or whoever." Sri Lanka, Boris. But thanks for calling. (2006)

. . .

Hundreds of wilting red roses from the Chelsea Flower Show were put to good use by innovative members of Conservative Future, the modern-day equivalent of the Young Conservatives. The youthful pinstripe brigade handed out the tired blooms at Sloane Square underground station to travellers with a little handwritten message: "Labour's red rose has let you down." Not one visitor refused their kind offer. (2004)

. . .

A home office mole reports a new system devised by senior civil servants there for reading the mood of their secretary of state, William Whitelaw. It involved counting the number of times he says "dear, dear" in reply to any remark, suggestion, news or proposal. There were fears for his life the other day when he was heard to utter no fewer than 21 successive "dears". But his staff were most understanding: the reason for his dismay was a memo from the PM. (1980)

Ann Widdecombe was paddling in her office in the state-of-the-art 1 Parliament Street building after water poured down from the fifth floor, bypassed the fourth floor that houses Labour MPs, gushed into Widders's office on the third floor and missed the second floor – also home to Labour MPs. "It's like Noah's Ark in here," wailed La Widdecombe. "It is definitely a Labour leak." *(2004)*

. . .

Apropos Lord Butler and the lobby system, both of which have received some scrutiny this week – the first because he died, the second because it lives – our political editor recalls the first advice he was given when he was a raw freshman at Westminster. It came from Lawrence Thompson, lobby correspondent of the *News Chronicle*, and was: "There are two rules to remember. The first is never to believe anything Rab Butler tells you. The second is never to ignore anything Rab Butler tells you." *(1982)*

. . .

I do not know whether there is a Dirty Tricks Department in the Conservative party working to smear Labour leaders, as Labour officials are reported to believe. But if the Conservatives are thinking of establishing one, they have on their payroll a man with the experience to lead it. He is Christopher Patten, aged 30, now director of the Conservative Research Department and formerly personal assistant to Lord Carrington. In 1965, just after he left Oxford, he went to New York to help John Lindsay in his successful campaign for mayor. "I was working on what we called the filth section," he was reported as saying at the time. "My job was to dig up facts about our opponents."[8] *(1974)*

---

[8] Patten was elected in 1979 and as party chairman received much credit for John Major's government being re-elected in 1992, although he lost his own seat in the process.

Travelling first-class from Peterborough to London the other day, a friend found herself opposite a wiry-haired fellow whom she was convinced was Sir Keith Joseph. Unable to contain her curiosity, she scribbled "Is that Sir Keith Joseph?" on the corner of her newspaper, and passed it to the passenger on her right. He passed it back with a message of his own: "Yes, and I'm Patrick Jenkin."[9] (1984)

• • •

As Tory morale collapses (There are Cumbrian cattlesheds containing cheerier inmates than Conservative Central Office just now) the party's canvassing call centre has resorted to desperate measures. A CCO circular at the weekend tried to gee up flagging spirits as follows: "Yesterday Boris Johnson, Editor of *The Spectator* and PPC for Henley, helped to make a record 8,000 calls in one day!" This is quite a surprise. Boris not only speaks quite slowly, but stammers in a foppish sort of a way and rarely stays on a single subject for the length of a sentence. How many of these 8,000 exhortations can he really have made? "It's not like that," a senior gap-toothed flunky told me. "The idea is to use VIP visits to recruit volunteers, and inspire them to better efforts." And why was Boris's visit so successful? "He's quite scary," my GTF admits. "I dare say the people on the phones got their heads down and made calls because they were afraid of being introduced." (2001)

---

[9] Joseph was education secretary at the time; Jenkin was environment secretary.

There is a new terror stalking the House of Commons known as Redwood-Lite. Walking like a mummy from a Hammer film, it sneaks up behind Tory MPs, touches them on the arm and with a smile fixed as though with a coat-hanger tries to make small-talk. "John was so glum after losing the leadership campaign," says one victim of his icy touch, "that he is now trying to be more friendly and overdoing it." (1997)

"We're losing height! Play the Prime Minister's speech again!"

SHORT AND SWEET

As a fan of puns, I enjoyed this letter in *Country Life* from a reader in Kent: "While walking through the bluebell woods at Godinton, I came across an old microwave oven dumped close to the lane. I wonder if this is the first cooker of spring." (2015)

. . .

One of my readers rang directory inquiries the other day for the number of Jesus College, Oxford, only to be asked. "How are you spelling Jesus?" (1983)

. . .

The *Stockport Express*, announcing their charming child contest, suggests: "Have your child shot for Mother's Day." (1977)

. . .

Alastair Stewart, the ITN newsreader, is an aficionado of Eurovision. "The Greek singer can hold a note," he tweeted approvingly on Saturday. "Unlike the Greek central bank." (2015)

. . .

An advertisement in the *Evening Echo* of Basildon offers: "Smoker's chair, solid ash". (1976)

. . .

A notice spotted in a Greenwich newsagent's window: "To Goldie, my extremely clever labrador. If you are reading this please come home now. Dennis." (2014)

The Countryside Commission are moving in September from London to Cheltenham, which seems appropriate enough. Sadly, though, three quarters of the staff of 80 have declined to move with them, because they do not want to live in the country. (1974)

• • •

A Christmas cracker of a joke from the poet Ian McMillan. "I didn't enjoy being the writer-in-residence at the opticians," he says. "Nobody ever read the last line of my poems." (2015)

• • •

In the lavatory of a North London pub, a graffitist has written: "Apathy is the curse of Britain." Underneath, someone has added: "Who cares?" (1975)

• • •

Joke of the day from Gyles Brandreth, the former Tory MP: "I met a girl at a party, who told me she's taken up meditation. I told her it was better than sitting around doing nothing." (2014)

• • •

La Senza, the lingerie company, has gone into administration. There's an item for the news in briefs. Unless it turns out to be a storm in a D cup. (2014)

• • •

Least surprising news of the month comes in a press release: "Collecting paper money has become amazingly popular recently." (1975)

Final section on a ruled wine order list I have just received from a firm in Bradford, Yorkshire: "For internal use only." (1967)

. . .

The *Surrey Comet* carries a funeral directors' advertisement offering "a complete service to any destination". I always thought the choice of route was taken out of our hands. (1978)

. . .

Notice in Alitalia's Regent Street window: "We regret any inconvenience to our passengers caused by the modernisation of our ticket agency." (1971)

. . .

Two signs, side by side, in a church porch in Suffolk: "This is the House of God and the gate to heaven" and "This door will be locked during the winter". (1972)

. . .

Sebastian Coe[10] explaining the genesis of his talent: "If you lived in Sheffield and were called Sebastian, you had to learn to run fast at a very early age." (1998)

---

[10] Winner of four Olympic medals at 800 and 1,500 metres. Later a Tory MP and peer. Currently President of the IAAF (International Association of Athletics Federations).

BARRY FANTONI

'In the old days you had to be in a
West End play to do this in public'

SEX

A year ago, the Conservative conference opened to the news that Brooks Newmark, MP for Braintree, had been sending intimate photos of himself to what turned out to be a tabloid reporter rather than some floozy. James Cleverly succeeded him in the Essex constituency and told me this week that Newmark's shrunken majority had overshadowed his selection meeting. One stately Tory dowager approached Cleverly after the association had made their choice and congratulated him on being an impressive candidate. Then she grabbed his arm, leant in and whispered: "But if you ever get your c••• out, I'll hack it off with a machete." Cleverly had no doubt that she owned one and knew how to wield it. (2015)

• • •

A stern warning for journalists who turned up for the press launch of ITV2's steamy and controversial new prostitute drama, *Belle de Jour*, which stars Billie Piper. "Billie will be taking questions about nudity, prostitution and whipping," announced a flunky. "But you may not ask her about her private life." (2007)

• • •

Cricket news and South Africa's innings in the one-day international in Bloemfontein yesterday began with David Willey bowling to Quinton de Kock. If only the commentator Brian Johnston, who revelled in smutty jokes, were still alive. (2016)

• • •

There are many who, for all the efforts of EL James, prefer M&S to S&M. Joseph Connolly told a story about one of them at the launch of his twelfth novel, *Style*. Connolly's friend, so he claims, is married to a woman who is into *Fifty Shades of Grey*, the bestselling erotic novel. One day, she asked her husband to tie her up. This done, she whispered, "Tell me something dirty", to which the baffled man replied: "Er, the dishes?" Undaunted, his passionate wife looked him in the eyes and said: "I am in your power. You can do whatever you want tonight." At this, so Connolly says, the relieved chap hurried off to the Garrick. (2015)

• • •

Conjugal rights for prisoners may be the issue that prevents John Prescott from ever usurping Jack Straw as home secretary, as many in Westminster believe he would sorely like to do. According to Colin Brown's new biography of Labour's deputy leader, Prescott's support for free love in jail has made him the prison warder's foe.

The sight of cons conjoining with their spouses has always been enough to make a screw slam down on his dinner tray. In 1976, however, as MP for Kingston-upon-Hull, the ever-conscientious Prescott thought it a disgrace that prisoners were denied marital sex. "Sexual deprivation," he told the government of the day, "must surely constitute one of the worst and particularly most harmful aspects of loss of liberty. These are the processes which produce frustration and tension."

When the prisoners heard of his campaign, Prescott instantly became a prison pin-up. For the warders, however, he was a troublemaker. So when he turned up at his local jail one day to expound on his sex-for-all theme, they took revenge. Noticing that the tax disc on his car was out of date, they tipped off the police and Prescott was duly fined. (1996)

Heard at Newry magistrates' court, a young counsel applied for a variation of a bail order on behalf of his client. "On what grounds?" asked the magistrate. "It's interfering with his sex life, your honour," came the reply. There was a pause, then the magistrate said: "I thought these things were attached to the ankle." (2015)

· · ·

The news that John Whittingdale had a fling with a dominatrix who lived in west London has been sympathetically received. "What is London coming to," *The Spectator* asks in a leading article, "if an MP has to travel all the way to Earl's Court for such services, when they used to be available a stone's throw away from the Commons?" (2016)

· · ·

A Liberal Democrat MP has been mistaken for a lady of the night. Jenny Tonge, the party's international development spokeswoman, last week found herself ordered "off the streets" and accused of being a "bloody trollop" as she innocently went about her business in Westminster.

Jenny, 59, was relatively unfazed by her detractor, whom she dismissed as a "dotty old man". "I was wearing flat shoes and a long mac – so was he, now I come to think of it," she tells me. "I couldn't have looked less like a bloody trollop. I'm a late to middle-aged woman!" In fact, the member for Richmond Park rather enjoyed the barracking. "I like being called a trollop," she adds. "I have a track record of this I'm afraid."

A sordid past, then? Happily, it is all quite innocent. Dr Tonge was referring to a meeting she had arranged with Paul Dacre, the editor of the *Daily Mail*, in a Soho bar. "I spent an hour waiting for him in what turned out to be a knocking shop. I was getting very odd looks from people before I found out that I was supposed to be at the other end of the street." (2000)

• • •

Jonathan Aitken's ability to read and write made him popular with the lags when the disgraced former cabinet minister did time for perjury. "Each night a queue would form outside my cell asking me to help write letters home," he said. One showed his appreciation by offering the former chief secretary to the Treasury free rein of his library of hardcore pornography. As Aitken politely refused, the convict said: "Ah, well, if it's boys you're after …" and dived back into his collection. (2016)

• • •

Tony O'Reilly, the former baked beans magnate and proprietor of the *Independent* titles, was more than pleased to be presenting the Wedgwood World Master of Culinary Arts awards on Thursday night. He was just about to hand over to Nigella Lawson, who would dish out the first of the prizes, when his mind wandered elsewhere. "So, tonight, ladies and gentlemen, we're here to celebrate the best breasts – er, chefs, chefs…" Not everyone focused on the food in *Nigella Bites*, did they? (2002)

• • •

Claire Tomalin, the biographer of Pepys and Dickens, is fond of skinny-dipping. She writes in the latest *Cam*, the Cambridge alumni magazine, of a dinner at Emmanuel College after which she stripped and went for a swim in the fellows' pool. It clearly impressed the master of the college, the Chaucerian scholar Derek Brewer, who suggested to

Michael Frayn, her husband, that he apply to be his successor on the grounds that he had "a lively consort".

Tomalin says skinny-dipping "is a totally chaste activity in the dark". It reminds me of the story of Maurice Bowra, the Oxford classicist, who was bathing naked in the river with friends when a group came past. The others all covered their privates, but Bowra hid his head. "I don't know about you gentlemen," he said, "but in Oxford I am known by my face." (2015)

. . .

Three judges have been sacked for viewing pornography at work. What was their filth of choice? *Rumpy-pumpy of the Bailey*, suggested our cartoonist, but how about something modern, such as *50 Shades of Grayling*[11]? The gossip among m'learned friends is that their lascivious brethren were inspired by their boss's name. "When Igor Judge was lord chief justice, judges focused on judging," one tells me. "Now that John Thomas is in charge, they prefer to focus on their John Thomases." (2015)

. . .

Christina Odone has been fantasising about Peter Mandelson. Ms Odone the immaculate deputy editor of the *New Statesman*, writes about her ideal desert island experience in the *Erotic Review*, nominating Mandy as her luscious Man Friday.

---

[11] Chris Grayling was justice secretary from 2012-15. He was not popular with lawyers.

The piece – commissioned before his "outing" – sensuously heralds his arrival on her patch of sand: "A creature approaches the spot where I lie exhausted and trembling … Peter Mandelson," she pants, complaining that Mandy, in a leopard-skin loin-cloth, "looks bored" as she does the Dance of the Seven Veils. So she consults *Men are from Mars, Women are from Venus*, "trying to find clues as to my partner's lack of interest", until, as the sun sets, and after a "timid caress" (hers) Mandy says: "I don't like this" and asks: "Perhaps we could find a third way?"[12] (*1998*)

---

[12]   Peter Mandelson, the MP for Hartlepool and architect of New Labour's "Third Way" philosophy, placing the party between its roots and the Conservatives. In 1998, he was outed as gay by *The Times's* Matthew Parris on *Newsnight*. *Men are from Mars* etc was a popular counselling book published in 1992.

BARRY FANTONI

"The last time I asked, you said
your sales conference was in
Bradford"

ERRORS

The *Charlotte Observer* of North Carolina reported: "Princess Anne got a dressing gown in Parliament Thursday for her recent fox hunting expeditions." The *New Yorker*, which spotted the misprint, commented: "Some of those English foxes are quite informal." (1973)

. . .

Bridegroom Ben Gooder, featured in the society wedding pages of *Tatler*, admits his promising City career was cut short by a most unfortunate misunderstanding. On the basis of a telephone call he bought 500 "most expensive shares" for a client who, in fact, wanted 500 Marks & Spencer shares. (1992)

. . .

An unfortunate typo from the Royal British Legion's Twitter account during the VE-Day concert on Saturday. According to the tweet, Alfie Boe, the tenor, sang *You'll Never Walk Again*. (2015)

. . .

David Lammy, the one-time culture minister, struggled on *Celebrity Mastermind*. He failed to identify the highest tier of theatre seating as "the gods" and suggested that the cheese often eaten with port was Red Leicester rather than Stilton. But Lammy's tour de force was his assertion that the monarch who succeeded Henry VIII was "Henry VII". Lammy is now minister for higher education and intellectual property. (2009)

A *Times* man who was in Berlin in 1945 retrieved a painting signed by Adolf Hitler from the ruins of the bunker. He took it and on his way out met an American sergeant whose prize was cutlery marked "AH". They compared booty and the sergeant so coveted the painting that our man, judging the spoons and forks the better bet, agreed to swap. A few days later he found the cutlery had come from the Adlon Hotel. (1983)

. . .

Events in Crimea brought back memories for Professor Michael Boulter, the palaeobotanist, of being in Czechoslovakia when the Soviet Union invaded to crush the uprising of 1968. With jets roaring overhead and tanks rumbling through the streets, Boulter bolted, taking care to protect a 30-million-year-old fossilised seed he had found. They made it safely back to Heathrow, where a customs officer demanded he open the fossil's case. "Unfortunately the fellow then sneezed and, well, that was the end of it." (2014)

. . .

The Midland Bank's staff magazine recounts how their regional head office in Manchester attempted to telephone the Bank of England's Manchester branch in its new premises. The number had been changed and directory enquiries said they could not help. When it was suggested that surely the Bank of England would be on the telephone, the imperturbable co-operator in inquiries said: "You've probably got the wrong name – they'll be one of those banks that have recently been taken over by someone else". (1972)

Today is Shakespeare Day. Jeremy Hornsby, a retired *Daily Express* hack, recalled having to write a piece about the playwright for the 350th anniversary of his death in 1966. "Can you get me *Timon of Athens*?" he shouted to his secretary, to which she replied: "Who's that? Our new stringer in Greece?" (2016)

· · ·

Fun scenes, we are told, at St Stephen's entrance to the Houses of Parliament, as Bill Gates and entourage are told "you're not on our list" by police and are forced to queue up and pass through security with hoi polloi. A glitch in the Westminster security computer, perhaps? Was it running Windows? (2008)

· · ·

A frowning Ed Balls appeared in the Commons yesterday for his first grilling by the Children, Schools and Families select committee, only to be informed gravely that a colour was missing from the rainbow on the cover of his Children's Plan policy document.

Pink, the minister conceded.

"Indigo!" chorused the room.

"Oh," a puzzled Balls said. "I was using the song." (2008)

Sometimes you just couldn't make it up with John Prescott. On the *Today* programme on Radio 4 yesterday clarifying the tectonic plates comment, he said: "Get your quotes right, John." He was being interviewed by Jim Naughtie.[13] (2004)

. . .

A puzzle in this week's *Observer Magazine*. In a question-and- answer survey on whether the Queen should abdicate in favour of Prince Charles, it carried a response from "Lord Egremont, former private secretary to Sir Harold Macmillan". The attribution of a knighthood to the former premier was corrected in the main paper, but nowhere was it mentioned that Lord Egremont, whom they appeared to have questioned on the matter, died in 1972. (1976)

. . .

Lord Cudlipp[14] has had his first postcard from his granddaughter, who is touring the Soviet Union: Yesterday, she writes, "we went to see Lennon's tomb". (1983)

. . .

Asked on his first US chat show what he did for fun in Australia, a young Heath Ledger[15] replied: "Me and my mates like to grab our weenies and sit around in thongs watching girls go by." The producers swiftly

---

[13] Prescott, the deputy prime minister, had described rumblings that Tony Blair might leave Downing Street as the shifting of tectonic plates. He assumed he was speaking to John Humphrys.

[14] Hugh Cudlipp was editor of the *Daily Mirror* in the 1950s. Made a peer in 1974. John Lennon, of the Beatles, was murdered in 1980, but in New York rather than Moscow.

[15] Actor, Oscar-nominated star of *Brokeback Mountain* (2005)

cut to commercials. In Australia thongs are flip-flops and weenies are hotdogs. "It was a long time before I got booked on another," says Ledger. (2006)

. . .

Ann Widdecombe, the saintly shadow home secretary, went to Bournemouth this week with a BBC film crew to discover whether the age of chivalry is dead. It's clearly very much alive on the South Coast. Widdecombe was walking down a street with the crew to try to see whether men still walked on the kerb side when they were with a woman, when she was approached by a tousle-haired youngster as the cameras were rolling.

"Hey, Missus," he said, "what's the programme about?"

"Manners," replied Widdecombe.

"Oh, sorry," said the blushing lad. "I should have said: excuse me, Miss, can you please tell me what the programme is about?" (2003)

. . .

A global email has been sent round the BBC that reads: "Unsure about where to put the apostrophe in 'its'? Confused about plurals and possessives? Bewildered by the difference between a comma and a semi-colon? Get to grips with punctuation and grammar with our new shame-free guide to the written language." The message gives more details of the course and ends: "If your interested let me know." (2001)

Detention is in order for Nigel de Gruchy, general secretary of the National Association of Schoolmasters and Union of Women Teachers. Yesterday *The Times* reported his attack on government plans to sack teachers if their pupils perform badly: "To call this measure Victorian or draconian is an insult to Victoria and Dracula." Er, what? "Doesn't Dracula come from Draconian?" asked a confused De Gruchy yesterday. Had there been more classics in schools, he might have known about Draco, the ancient Athenian legislator. "Perhaps I should have stuck to Victoria," he conceded. (1997)

• • •

This year's runner-up in the *Cosmopolitan* New Journalist of the Year competition, Jane White, was a real hit with editor Linda Kelsey. She loved Jane's sensitive piece on today's ideal man. All in all she "epitomised the quintessential *Cosmo* woman – intelligent, witty and feminine". So it was a shock to Ms Kelsey when Jane arrived to claim her prize and revealed her true identity: Liverpool van driver Kevin Sampson. (1986)

"Bloody voters! They're only in it for themselves"

LOCAL POLITICS

Baroness Trumpington, the delightful battleaxe, is going stronger than ever at 90. She says that when she worked in local government she was taken to visit a stud farm at Newmarket, where she was told that stallions become very frisky at the scent of a mare. "Good heavens," she said, making quickly for the exit. "I'm a mayor and I'm wearing scent." (2013)

• • •

Linguistic vandalism from Wolverhampton council, which has changed the name of its anti-vandalism committee to "the urban conservation and environmental awareness working party". (1981)

• • •

An architect employed by one of the London boroughs had a perspective drawing of a housing development scheme returned by his superior the other day. The complaint? That the skirt lengths of the female figures in the drawing were two inches too short. (1967)

• • •

Nice to see that venerable British traditions are being maintained in Oxfordshire. Reporting the cold snap, the *Oxford Times* has two local depots saying that "some of their gritters were temporarily out of action because of the freezing weather". (1977)

• • •

What do you get for the man who has everything except a public convenience in Lewisham? Fortunately, Lewisham borough council has the answer. Advertising in this week's *Estates Gazette*, the council offers "for alternative uses" the now vacant ladies and gents on the South Circular. Have they had any takers yet? "Interest has been pretty good," reports a spokesman. "The main interest is converting it into office space; a few have suggested using it as an artist's studio or maybe a coffee shop. It's all cisterns go." (2001)

• • •

Barbara Castle, "as one who has campaigned for equal toilet facilities for women for many years", lent her support to a petition signed by more than 100 of her lady neighbours in Islington. The petitioners asked that the ladies' public conveniences in Highbury Crescent, which the council had closed for winter, should be re-opened. The neighbouring men's lavatories, it was pointed out, were still in operation.

Mrs Castle wrote personally to the leader of Islington borough council about the matter – which was duly discussed in the public services committee. Such discrimination between the sexes, it was agreed, was quite intolerable but the outcome was not quite what Mrs Castle and the incensed Islingtonian sorority had hoped. Now the gents' conveniences will be closed for the winter too. (1969)

• • •

As part of a crime prevention survey, Islington council's police committee has asked house-holders to fill in a questionnaire giving details of total family income and times when people are out. Then, say the instructions, "put it in the plastic bag and leave it on your doorstep. It will be collected in the morning." You bet. (1985)

Have we all missed a major news story? "Council has received the resignation of Mrs Thatcher with very real regret; it has left her place vacant for the time being. Meanwhile it has co-opted Mr Heath." Well, it was a big story for the Aylmerton and Runton parish magazine in Norfolk, reporting changes on Runton parochial church council. (1980)

. . .

Tory MEP Lord Bethell was last week in Prague, where Czech democrats were enormously impressed with the glamour and power of the European parliament. Bethell agreed about the institution's importance, but had to tell them that not everyone in the West shared their view. He cited as an example the north London constituent who rang him asking him to do something about an infestation of rats. When Bethell asked whether the caller had contacted the health inspector at the local town hall, his constituent explained that he had not wanted to bother anyone so important. (1990)

. . .

Five Tory councillors in South Wales now talk proper because Conservative Central Office has paid £100 for them to have a ten-week elocution course. Katherine Edwards, their teacher, diagnosed grammar defects, dropped aitches and chronic Cardiff accents, certainly severe weaknesses in a party led by the lord high elocutioner herself.

Week after week, the Dai Doolittles were made by their young lady Higgins to stand at one end of a room, like men before a firing squad, and clear their vowels by reciting time and again: "Father's car is a Jaguar, and Pa drives very fast. Castles, farms and draughty barns, we all go charging past." (1979)

Cornwall county council may be about to return unopened a gift from Prince Charles. To celebrate the birth of his second son, the Prince in his capacity as Duke of the Duchy of Cornwall presented the council with Kit Hill on Bodmin Moor. Councillors were appropriately moved by his generosity until they learnt that the hill needs £37,000 spent immediately on scrub clearing and fencing and will cost nearly £12,000 a year to keep up. "What gets up my nose", exploded Liberal councillor John Scannell, "is that the Duchy retains the mineral rights." (1985)

• • •

The village of Hadleigh in Essex has fallen 514 years behind in paying rent for an old building. The rent agreed by the landlord, Sir William Clopton, in 1439 was only a single red rose per annum, but these things add up. Sir William's heir, American businessman Gene Clopton, has worked out that with interest the village owes him 1,303,364 roses. Generously he has decided to settle for just one. Pushing his luck, the mayor of Hadleigh, Christopher Culpin, has invited Clopton to a rent-paying ceremony this month – when he hopes to raise other matters, such as landlord liability for repairs and improvements. (1984)

*"Crikey! It's Thursday — I'm
down to fight for the other side."*

FORTUNES
OF WAR

Leo McKinstry, who has written a book about how Britain repelled Germany's Operation Sea Lion in the Second World War, told a story at an *Oldie* lunch about a Home Guardsman who came across an amorous couple in a parked car. Tapping on the driver's window, he declared: "You've entered a prohibited area." From the passenger seat came the swift reply: "Oh no he hasn't." (2014)

• • •

Harpers & Queen has a serendipitously commissioned piece on female war reporters in the new issue. The mag went to press before the current "war" started, so I dare say they are delighted. The piece opens with the conventional image of a lady war reporter (in this case Marie Colvin[16]) drinking strong black coffee (they always do, you know) but it is the second sentence that really gets things moving. "She probably needs my early morning visit like she needs a hole in the head," it says. A cliché as clunky as that would be gross at the best of time; it is particularly grim when you consider that, when shrapnel from a Tamil Tiger grenade hit poor Marie in the eye in Sri Lanka in April, a hole in the head is exactly what she got. (2001)

• • •

Napoleon the Great? Not according to the historian Adam Zamoyski, who argued with Andrew Roberts at an Intelligence Squared debate that the Corsican despot wasn't all that impressive. As one example, Zamoyski referred to Napoleon losing his virginity to a prostitute but said that she was the fourth one that he had tried to purchase. "Now excuse me," he said, "but if a young officer cannot pick up a tart I don't see that as some mark of a great achiever." (2014)

[16] An award-winning Sunday Times war correspondent for more than 25 years, Colvin was killed while covering the civil war in Syria in 2012.

Charlemagne, it appears, had strong views on mini-skirts. Mr J N L Myres, formerly Bodley's librarian at Oxford, recalls in the June issue of *Antiquity* a brief passage about the ninth-century vogue for "brevissima palliola" in the Monk of St Gall's biography of Charlemagne. The mini-skirts were introduced by the Frisians, who then controlled the rag trade. At first Charlemagne did not forbid the new fashion, because it seemed quite suitable for warlike exercises. But when he learnt that the Frisians were selling them at the same price as they had sold maxi-skirts, he ordered that no one should buy from them anything at the customary price except the most ample and lengthy garments. "What is the use of these skimpy little things anyway?" Charlemagne asked. "When I am in bed they don't cover me properly; when I am on horseback they don't protect me against the wind and rain: and when I retire for the purposes of nature my legs are so frozen that I cannot do anything." (1968)

• • •

My colleague John Witherow, just back from the Falklands, tells me that journalists expended almost as much energy trying to get off the islands once the hostilities had finished as they did in covering the war. So anxious were they to leave that they considered such desperate measures as chartering a seaplane from Chile, boarding a hospital ship to Montevideo or even sneaking off with Argentine prisoners in the *Canberra*. Rivalry reached its peak in the struggle to secure a place on the first Hercules aircraft bound for Ascension. The lucky few got seats after a straw poll, and in the face of stiff SAS opposition. (1982)

Gawain Towler, Nigel Farage's former spin doctor, who almost became an MEP last month, tells a good story of when he was training at Sandhurst and was told by his commanding officer: "They'll follow you, Towler. Not out of loyalty, but morbid curiosity." (2014)

. . .

As a result of the abolition of the Navy's rum tot, Admiral Sir Michael le Fanu, first sea lord and chief of naval staff, who has always been known through the Fleet as "Ginger", is now being referred to as "Dry Ginger". (1969)

. . .

General Sir Michael Gow, former head of the Royal College of Defence Studies, hung up his epaulettes six weeks late. A few days before he was due to retire, he slipped while running for a train at Waterloo station and broke his ankle. Since regulations forbid an officer to retire while in hospital, he was obliged to continue drawing full pay until the injury healed. Some compensation, perhaps, for being the last general to fall at Waterloo. (1986)

. . .

A military historian friend of mine has unearthed an astonishing story of how Lord Cardigan's role in the Charge of the Light Brigade was doctored to make it more heroic.

A war artist, William Simpson, went to the Crimea to sketch the action, but missed the charge. Eyewitnesses helped him to reconstruct it and he showed the sketch to Cardigan, the brigade commander, who snapped back at him: "It is all wrong." Simpson tried again, twice. The third time, Cardigan gave his approval because Simpson took great pains to make the commander conspicuous in front of the brigade. When Cardigan went to Windsor Castle to explain the charge to Queen Victoria, he took Simpson's watercolour with him. The queen remarked in her diary how Cardigan "spoke very modestly as to his own wonderful heroism". (1978)

• • •

When Red Adair starts tackling the blazing Kuwaiti oil wells, the military should avoid giving him daft orders. While the veteran troubleshooter was "killing" a fire at an American well some years ago, an oil company official made the mistake of insisting that Adair observe the rule that plastic safety hats must be worn at all times. "I took this dude down as close to the fire as he could stand it and stood there with him," says Adair. "I see your point," the official was forced to admit, as his hat started to melt and run down around his ears. (1991)

*"Tony's out of the country
so much he doesn't have to
pay UK tax."*

ON THE LEFT

Gordon Brown's stand-up career continues. On Saturday, the former prime minister returned to Edinburgh University, his alma mater, where he reflected on his brief time as a lecturer. "I found that universities stand for integrity, objectivity, impartiality for the search for truth and the pursuit of knowledge," he said. "These were all qualities I had to leave behind when I went into politics." (2014)

. . .

Throughout his 13-year career in the House of Commons, Eric Moonman, the former Labour MP for Basildon, never saw his name on an early day motion. Now that he is chairman of Islington health authority, the situation has changed: Jeremy Corbyn, Labour MP for Islington North, mentioned Moonman by name in a motion that is highly critical of the authority. Moonman thinks the absurdity of these motions is plumbing new depths. A recent one put down by an MP for debate congratulated the winners of a football match. "Someone should look at the cost of printing this sort of thing," says Moonman. "It seems to me that if we're not careful, early day motions could be used as a substitute for a congratulatory telegram service."[17] (1983)

. . .

Jeremy Corbyn's long march from the People's Republic of North Islington is going well, but he is not universally loved among his tribe. A reception was thrown in Westminster a few years ago for David Choquehuanca, the Bolivian chancellor, at which Corbyn was seen having a long conversation with the star guest through a translator. One senior Labour MP on the hard left of the party was overheard

---

[17]   This was the first mention in the Diary of Corbyn, who a mere 32 years later would become a surprising leader of the Labour party. Until then, he was best known for signing increasingly loopy Commons motions

declaring: "I'd have thought that huanca could understand the other huanca perfectly without the aid of any translation." (2015)

. . .

Roy Hattersley, who is being challenged for his job as Labour's deputy leader, backed his car into a concrete no-parking bollard at the Commons yesterday. He did not get out to see what he had hit. "It's a keep-left sign," shouted Ron Brown, the MP from Leith. (1988)

. . .

He was laid to rest in Highgate cemetery in 1883, but Karl Marx, the father of Communism, has been brought back to life. In the last bulletin of the Association of British Science Writers, his name appeared on a blacklist of members who failed to pay the correct subscription fee. (1996)

. . .

Around 50 grey-haired Labour MPs are resisting attempts to make new Labour the party of modern technology. Joe Ashton, the 66-year-old Bassetlaw MP, states their case: "I don't refuse to get email because I'm an old fogey. It's because I'm an old pro who knows the workload it would create. Teachers are the biggest problem. Any time their pupils are learning anything about the government they'll say: 'Write to your MP.' I get questionnaires by the dozen and if you don't answer them they think you're just a miserable old soul and their dad will never vote for you again." Surely not. (2000)

The late Denis Healey became a loveable old cove in retirement, but he had a reputation as a bully in his pomp. The former Tory MP Jerry Hayes recalls a conversation with Denzil Davies, who was a junior Treasury minister when Healey was chancellor of the exchequer. Davies said that he got fed up with being constantly called assorted Anglo-Saxon names by his boss in meetings and requested that they should interact only in writing. Did that work? Hayes asked. Davies sighed: "No, he just used to write t•••, w••••• and b••••••• in the margins of all his memos to me." (2015)

• • •

"Talking on a mobile phone while driving affects your concentration and ability to react," says Douglas Alexander, the transport secretary. "It is impossible to do two things at once and do them well." Douglas Alexander is also the Scottish secretary. (2007)

• • •

Jim Murphy is the frontrunner to be the next Scottish Labour leader, but he may struggle to find fans in parts of Glasgow. A few years ago Murphy played in a charity football match and, despite being a Celtic fan, was made to wear a Rangers shirt. A photograph of him celebrating after he scored a goal in the enemy kit did not go down well. Next time he was at Celtic Park a fan caught Murphy's attention in the usual way (by throwing a beer can at his head) and shouted: "Your family must be ashamed of you. Why couldn't you have been stealing your expenses like everybody else?" (2014)

At the funeral of President Ford yesterday this country was represented by Sir David Manning, the British ambassador to the US. Strange that Gordon Brown, for example, couldn't be persuaded to attend the funeral of this former head of government who stepped in unelected to replace a disgraced predecessor, served a mere two years and was then booted from office at the ballot box. Whatever could have put him off?[18] (2007)

. . .

Quote from Len Murray last week: "The TUC is not involved in party politics. Nor is its general secretary ... I hope that every trade unionist with a vote in Walsall, Workington and Newcastle will cast it next Thursday for the Labour candidate." (1976)

. . .

The pleasingly indiscreet former spin-doctor Alastair Campbell, in an article for the AOL website, describes the prime minister at a computer-skills class for adults in the North East. "The prime minister noticed that the man next to him seemed nervous, almost anxious," Campbell writes. "'I'm sorry you have to endure all this media glare just because you're next to me'," said Mr Blair. "'No,' came the reply, 'what's worrying me is that you're the prime minister, I'm long-term unemployed and I've done better than you in every single test'." (2006)

---

[18] Brown should not have been so pessimistic. He survived three years before being booted out of office.

I hear that the TUC and the Tory government are locked in an unusual embrace of cooperation to head off a potential embarrassment. Next Monday union leaders are due to visit the department of employment headquarters to unveil a centenary plaque to Ernest Bevin, founder of the TGWU and Churchill's minister of labour. Unfortunately, that very day civil servants are staging a one-day strike. Neither side wishes to soil the Bevin memory with the sight of the TUC general council crossing a picket line, and alternative plans are being hurriedly examined. (1981)

. . .

Labour deputy whip Norman Hogg may be having second thoughts about accepting an invitation to visit Malta – extended by the country's National party leader, Dr Leuis Galea, during a visit to the Commons this week. After promising to greet him personally, Galea added: "It would give me pleasure also to hospitalise you." (1985)

. . .

Arthur Scargill's[19] insistence that press calls to NUM headquarters all go to his office (though, of course, one never gets to speak to him) is causing difficulty now that he is holidaying in Cuba. "You can hold on if you like", I was told by a flummoxed telephonist, "but I cannot put you through until August 16." (1982)

---

[19] The militant leader of the National Union of Mineworkers

Ever the realist, Ken Livingstone[20] has come up with the ultimate solution to unemployment: make him prime minister. "If I was PM so many people would leave the country that there would be plenty of jobs to go round the few that were left," he told *National Student* magazine. (1986)

• • •

Pioneering 1920s feminist Dora Russell, now 89, in Blackpool to address a women's fringe meeting, complained to Glenys Kinnock[21] that she was fed up with people continually mentioning her husband, Bertrand Russell[22]. "I know what it's like," Glenys sympathised, to which Dora retorted, "Yes, but you didn't divorce your husband in 1932." (1984)

• • •

The prime minister paid his old friend (and rival) Gordon Brown a terrific compliment yesterday at a rally in London. "He's the best chancellor Britain's had this century," Tony Blair trilled. I wonder if he'll be saying that tomorrow, on day 22 of the century. (2000)

• • •

Peter Mandelson revealed in an after-dinner speech at a West London synagogue that when Tony Blair announced Cherie's pregnancy, Robin Cook was in an international conference and hadn't been informed. The then foreign secretary was therefore rather bemused

---

[20] At the time, the hard-left leader of the Greater London Council. He became an MP the next year.

[21] Wife of the Labour leader at the time, Neil Kinnock.

[22] Philosopher, social critic and winner of the Nobel Prize for literature.

when Bertie Ahern[23] bounded up to him and expressed his delight about Tony's "great news".

Cook scratched his beard and wandered what Ahern was going on about. Perhaps there had been a major breakthrough in the peace process? He decided to flannel until he was better briefed and told Ahern: "I'm very happy to hear the news. You wouldn't believe how hard Tony worked for that. He's been trying for ages." (2002)

• • •

Some of our political dinosaurs are already extinct in the minds of the young. The new, very green, puppet co-ordinator on *Spitting Image* was sent to collect the latex version of Arthur Scargill from a storeroom. "What does he look like?" she asked. The producer, Giles Pilbrow, told her: "You can't miss him, he's an old, balding, left-wing Labour politician with a grubby grey suit." She returned with Neil Kinnock. (1996)

• • •

Labour became the last of the three main parties to unveil its election theme tune yesterday – a specially written piece by Michael Kamen, who seems to delight in composing tunes to accompany punitive tax policies. His last major commission was the score for *Robin Hood: Prince of Thieves*. (1992)

---

[23] Irish Taoiseach, 1997-2008

Don't give your girlfriend flowers on Valentine's Day. Give her an annual subscription to the Labour Party. That, at least, is what Labour would like you to do. Determined to increase its membership, the party has designated February 14 as its first national Recruit-a-Friend day. To ram the point home, it will be inserting appropriately worded messages in the Valentine's Day columns of the national newspapers. It has drawn the line at one suggestion – "Get Your Lover into Labour" – but watch out for references to red roses and invitations to ring a freephone number. (1989)

McGONAGALL writes —

ODE to the SCOTTISH PARLIAMENT

"*O, wondrous building, pride of the Scottish nation! Costing only £40 million, plus 600% inflation!*"

SCOTLAND, WALES AND IRELAND

Sir Terry Wogan gave his first speech as president of the PG Wodehouse Society at their biennial dinner last week and said that, like Wodehouse, he had started his working life as an unhappy bank clerk. After he became a success in broadcasting, Wogan revisited his old branch in Limerick, where he met a former colleague. "Do you remember Sean O'Kelly, who joined the bank at the same time as you?" he was asked. "He's assistant manager in Tralee now. You left at the wrong time." (2014)

. . .

Five Welsh Labour MPs have been spending the summer recess conducting a private investigation into the likely impact that British entry into the Common Market will have on the principality. The result of their labours will appear tomorrow in the form of a 40-page booklet entitled *The Common Market and Wales*.

The five are John Morris (Aberavon), Bryn John (Pontypridd), Elystan Morgan (Cardiganshire), Neil Kinnock (Bedwellty) and Denzil Davies (Llanelli). Morris tells me that says the overall conclusion is that "entry would be a bad thing for the Principality". He adds: "We have all had the experience of trying to get new industry away from the centre. It is difficult enough when dealing with Whitehall but it will be even more difficult when decisions are taken even farther away in Brussels."[24] (1971)

---

[24] This is the first mention in the Diary of Kinnock, who led the Labour party from 1983-92. He clearly changed his opinion on the EU, since he went on to become vice-president of the European Commission while his wife, Glenys, served for 15 years as an MEP.

Lord Brooke of Sutton Mandeville, the former Northern Ireland Secretary, turned 80 a few days ago. Jerry Hayes, who worked under him as a junior MP, tells a story about Brooke's first day in the job, when he was shown a map of the province by his civil servants with areas colour-coded according to political allegiance. Orange for unionists, green for republicans and so on. "The blue bit is where the Conservatives are, I suppose?" he asked. "Not quite, minister," came the reply. "That's a lough." (2014)

• • •

The staid rites of the Scottish Conservative conference at Perth were disrupted enough by the catcalling, foot-stamping, bagpipe-playing and ballot-rigging accusations surrounding the anti-devolution campaign. To add to it, there was an effort to introduce American-style razzmatazz, but it did not work very well. When the traditional ecstatic ovation for Margaret Thatcher was at its height on Saturday a team of female Young Conservatives trotted to the front and held up placards before the audience spelling out ASSEMBLY OK.

Phase two of the manoeuvre came when they faced the opposite way to show Mrs Thatcher, Lord Home of the Hirsel and the other dignitaries their legend. No one apparently realized that this meant Mrs Thatcher had to stare baffled at the runic words: KO YLBMESSA. It was said that this ploy was the work of Michael Ancram, an engaging party vice-chairman of 31 appointed to smarten up-public relations and who once attended a Democratic convention in the United States. I expect it was the year the Democrats lost.[25] (1976)

---

[25] Ancram went on to spend 27 years as an MP, including as deputy leader of the party and shadow foreign secretary. He now sits in the Lords as the Marquess of Lothian.

David Norris, an Irish politician and equal-rights campaigner, was awarded the lifetime achievement prize at the annual *Pink News* bash at the Foreign and Commonwealth Office on Wednesday. He said in his speech that the acoustics were much better at the FCO than when he had addressed an awards gala at the Natural History Museum. "I made some inquiries and discovered that I could be heard only if I spoke inside the skeleton of the diplodocus," he said. "As a politician I've often been accused of talking through my arse, but this was the first time I've spoken through the arse of a dinosaur." (2015)

• • •

A banner declaring "I love porn" was ripped down from the entrance to the Students Union at Cardiff University the other day. The reason? Rather than displaying an abhorrence of pornography, students were outraged that the proclamation was not also written in Welsh. A union law dictates that only bilingual signs should be given the stamp of approval. (2000)

• • •

The sport of kings has been hit by a plague of marauding rabbits that forced the cancellation of two steeplechase races at Down Royal racetrack in Co Antrim, Northern Ireland. An inspection found that rabbits had dug hundreds of yards of warren directly under the racecourse, prompting fears that the pounding of hooves could cause the collapse of the track. A rabbit-proof boundary was erected after the problem emerged 15 years ago, but the bunnies are back. The bookmaker Paddy Power is offering odds of 100-1 that the racecourse will change its name to Watership Down Royal. If it does, who better to cut the ribbon at the opening ceremony than the leader of the Irish Labour Party, one Pat Rabbitte? (2004)

At last it can be told how Dublin was saved from drought by the private parts of King William of Orange's horse. The steed, Chillaby, bore the monarch in an equestrian statue, which stood in College Green until 1929, when republicans blew it up. King Billy and what remained of his horse were carted to a junkyard and forgotten, until the Second World War when Dublin was having great difficulties maintaining water supplies. Thousands of gallons a day were being lost through cracks in ageing pipes and lead for repairs was hard to find. It was then that an engineer noticed Chillaby's private parts. In this respect the horse was well-endowed. He had about a stone and half of them. Quick examination proved they were made of lead. Chillaby was gelded at once, and the lead used to patch the pipes. Confirming the story, a corporation spokesman said the authorities had first been asked what had happened to the monument ten years ago, but had been too embarrassed to tell the truth. (1982)

• • •

The citizens of Edinburgh may have an attitude that is often described as "fur coats and nae knickers" but it seems that the desperate marketing of Harvey Nichols in Scotland's capital is taking it a bit too far. Last week the top people's store held a bingo evening in the restaurant and it has now announced that it will hold pole-dancing lessons in-store. There is a danger of making Topshop look upmarket. (2004)

• • •

A Press Association report of the proposed meeting of revolutionary groups in Ireland noted that the last time a similar get-together was planned, some delegates were turned away at British ports. "This time, though," the report says, "they will be advised to travel incognito as ordinary terrorists." That should be all right then.[26] (1976)

---

[26] Surely this was an error and for terrorists we should read tourists?

John Costello, the former Irish prime minister whose obituary we published yesterday, endeared himself to the Washington press in a splendidly Irish incident. Visiting the US capital in 1956, he had begun a speech to the National Press Club when an aide tugged his coat. "They've just told me that I've been giving you the wrong speech," Costello told his audience. "The one meant for the senators this afternoon." Then he launched into the correct one. What pleased the reporters most was that the speech for them was notably the more erudite. (1976)

• • •

Ian Paisley's lack of German has landed Northern Ireland secretary Tom King with an unfortunate new image. Intending to liken him to Hitler's propagandist, recently, the ranting cleric mispronounced Goebbels as Gerbils – a mistake repeated in the *Observer*'s report. One of the Unionist protestors now constantly dogging King's footsteps has shown a rare degree of wit for their number. He turns up with a placard caricature – not of the Nazi propaganda chief but of the furry little rodent. (1986)

• • •

I have been keeping my word and watching the World Cup mainly on ITV, but I have switched over to the BBC from time to time to see what their experts are wearing. I note that where they have tartan jackets for the Scottish games on ITV, they merely sport tartan ties on BBC, which shows which side takes its responsibilities more seriously. (1974)

"At least he won't get lost
in the desert"

EMBARRASSMENTS

As the author of novels that rarely top a few hundred pages, it is a little surprising to hear Ian McEwan[27] claim that modern works are too long. Yet his son, Greg, may argue that even McEwan's novels are too lengthy, or at least too ambiguous. Speaking at Cadogan Hall in London, the author recalled that his son studied *Enduring Love* at A level and received an hour-long exegesis from his father on the meaning behind the story. Though it came from the author's mouth, Greg's teachers were unimpressed. "Apparently, the teacher disagreed with my analysis on political grounds," McEwan said. "The essay came back with a D." (2014)

• • •

John Prescott has gaffed again. During the course of a live BBC interview yesterday evening, the deputy prime minister offered a typically coherent resume of his house-building plans.

Bamboozled by the distinction between "single parents" and "single occupancy", Prescott asked: "Can we do that again? I made that crap." After a telling pause, the interviewer, Nick Robinson, spluttered: "Deputy prime minister, do you realise we are still live?" (2000)

• • •

Tatler has a feature this month on the most exclusive restaurants. One is Kensington Place in Notting Hill, which likes to bring snooty customers down a peg or two. Bruce Oldfield, the fashion designer, once rang them at 7pm and asked for a table. "I'm sorry, we're full," said the manager. "Surely you keep a table or two for celebrities?" Oldfield said, haughtily. "Yes," the manager conceded. "Who are you bringing?" (2016)

---

[27] Winner of the Booker Prize for *Amsterdam* in 1998. *Enduring Love* was published in 1997.

Andrew Marr, the BBC's political editor, was barred from the Houses of Parliament for several days after producing a fake Commons pass made by his son on a home computer.

An embarrassed Mr Marr had carried the mock pass in his wallet behind his real one for several months before it fell out while renewing his genuine pass last Wednesday.

Commons security staff, already on high alert because of the terrorist threat, decided to teach the journalist, one of the most senior at the BBC, a lesson. They confiscated both passes, forcing Mr Marr to broadcast from College Green opposite the Houses of Parliament, instead of from the Lobby where he normally operates. Mr Marr said: "One of my children mocked up a card in ten minutes on his laptop. I had to apologise and got it back this week." (2004)

• • •

The BBC has received a plea from a viewer of North West Tonight, who saw a report on terrorism. "You used footage of a shopping centre that shows a middle-aged couple," he wrote. "I am one of those people. Unfortunately, the woman I am with is not my wife. Is there any way that you can stop using this?" (2015)

• • •

Michael Fabricant, the Lichfield MP, recalls his selection meeting in 1991, when in response to the standard "is there anything embarrassing in your past that we should be aware of" question, he replied: "If there were, I'm hardly going to tell you." Stunned silence, nervous laughter and then they took a punt on him. Probably gave points for honesty.

Now, 23 years later, Fabricant has admitted something he could have confessed to. In the 1980s he sold radio equipment around the world and on a trip to Russia was asked if he could read the 4pm news bulletin on Radio Moscow's English language service as the regular man had suddenly taken ill (or been shipped off to a Gulag camp). With a contract in the balance, Fabricant agreed. His grin soon evaporated, though, as he had to read, live to the world, the words: "Margaret Thatcher, Britain's fascist and war-mongering leader..." For some reason, he left that off his CV. (2014)

. . .

A variant on the theme that policemen get younger as a man grows older. A lady in her early forties crossing a West End London street was surprised to be greeted by a policeman with a gesture of open arms. Taking a closer look at her, he dropped his arms smartly and said, in an apologetic tone of voice: "I do beg your pardon, madam, I took you for my aunt." (1966)

. . .

The star guest at the Engineering Employers' Federation dinner on Tuesday (we do all the glamorous gigs) was Chuka Umunna, the ambitious shadow business secretary, who let slip Labour's election campaign strategy. "We are faking a cost of living crisis," he declared, before looking embarrassed and then clarifying: "I mean, facing." (2014)

Dan Snow, the historian son of Peter, the BBC television presenter, reveals his worst "embarrassing Dad" moment. "My dad was once given boxer shorts for Christmas because it was felt, you know, he should get with the modern era and stop wearing Y-fronts. He thought they were shorts so he just walked down the high street with a pair of boxer shorts with the flap hanging wide open. I mean, it was just awful." (2009)

• • •

It pays to check before you tease. Terry Eagleton, the Marxist literary critic, was browsing in an Oxford bookshop when he thought he saw a distinguished philosophy don thumbing through a copy of *Philosophy Made Simple*. Sidling up, he murmured in his ear "That's a bit difficult for you, isn't it?" only to gasp as a total stranger turned to face him. Eagleton stammered an apology and fled but admits: "Somewhere there is a man who believes that people in Oxford are so obnoxiously elitist that they jeer openly at the efforts of total strangers to improve their minds." (2013)

• • •

The discovery of Donald Campbell's[28] body, along with his boat *Bluebird*, reminds me of a story the Earl of Arran, known as "Boofy", told in the mid-1960s when Campbell was breaking another land-speed record in Australia. Boofy got on a train and sat next to a woman he thought was Mrs Donald Campbell – but in fact was her mother-in-law, the widow of Sir Malcolm Campbell. When Lady Campbell remarked "Isn't it hot?" goofy Boofy replied "Not nearly as hot as where your husband is now!" (2001)

---

[28] British speed record-holder on land and water. He died in a crash on Coniston Water in 1967, but his vehicle, Bluebird, was not recovered until 2001. His father, Sir Malcolm, was also a speed record-holder, who died in 1948.

David Cameron misplaced his deft way with words while on holiday. At the North Devon Show yesterday, the prime minister told the Chivenor Military Wives Choir: "You get around a bit." Suddenly realising that could be taken the wrong way, he quickly added that he meant it in a purely professional sense, of course. A career as the next Duke of Edinburgh awaits. (2013)

• • •

A JP confesses to having found himself in an embarrassing situation. Seated comfortably to hear a speaker at a society of which he is a member, he heard the chairman include his name among those who had apologised for their inability to attend. The whole of the evening was spent, he adds, trying to remember whether he should have been presiding at another meeting. He is still not sure whether his diary has let him down. (1966)

• • •

A new fact sheet prepared by London's Ritz Hotel informs guests that the most unusual items their predecessors have left behind include black pearls, a diamond watch and a Mercedes. But their forgetfulness does not stop there. Terry Holmes, managing director, recounts: "I remember when a fairly wealth American family was staying in the hotel. When it was time to leave they packed up several limousines outside the hotel and drove off with all their retinue including a nanny. Imagine our surprise when we discovered they'd left their baby behind." (1993)

Two harassed mothers of large families were travelling on the London underground the other day, each with half a dozen small and rebellious children milling around her. The train stopped and as the door were about to close, one of the mothers had still not removed all her small charges from the train. A man in a bowler hat, eager to help, seized on the nearest child and deposited it on the station platform. The doors closed but to his horror he found himself faced by the outraged mother of the second contingent. He had thrown out the wrong child. (1966)

"There's more chance of catching an infection in hospital than catching a train"

HEALTH

The healthiest party of the year will be given appropriately enough, by Sir George Godber, when he retires as chief medical officer at the department of health and social security on November 30. The invitation states: "There will be no smoking, no alcohol, but, in compensation, tea and no speeches." (1973)

. . .

Did the government consult any actual medics while composing its NHS reforms? Jane Dacre, president of the Royal College of Physicians, may have discovered why the plans were so poorly received. Rushing from work to a meeting at the Department of Health, she was stopped by two security guards, whose scanners detected a stethoscope in her bag.

"What's that?" they asked. She explained that she was a doctor. "That's interesting," they replied. "We don't get many of those in here. (2014)

. . .

A sore point among civil servants will be debated at the annual conference of the 180,000-strong Civil and Public Services association, largest of the Civil Service unions, in the Isle of Man next week. A motion from the Wiltshire branch of – appropriately – the department of health and social security, calls for the issue of modern tissue toilet paper to replace the old-fashioned and hard paper stamped "Government property" on every sheet still in universal use. A supporting motion from Warrington calls for "official toilet paper of a soft texture". (1971)

An anti-smoking advertisement in *The Guardian* declares that "one third of all smokers will die". If the others achieve immortality, it might be worth starting. (1977)

. . .

Baron Young of Cookham, formerly plain old Sir George the bicycling baronet, has published an enjoyable anthology of his exploits over 40 years as an MP. He writes of the fear every minister has that one embarrassing typo could land them in the papers. As a junior health minister, he wrote a letter about hospitals that was meant to end by saying that "this administration's policy, in contrast to our predecessor's, is to promote bed management". Fortunately, Young spotted just in time that his typist had spelt bed with an "a". (2015)

. . .

When a New Zealand guest runner, Bryan Rose, made a spirited but unavailing challenge to finish first in the English cross-country championships at Norwich on Saturday, veteran followers of the sport brought up the name of Joseph Guillemot, of France, who in the early 1920s was the last foreigner to win what are now closed championships. Only a few are likely to remember that Guillemot made a special impact on a doctor busy with his stethoscope at the end of the 1920 race. The medical man turned deathly white when he discovered Guillemot's heart was apparently silent. Only after a few frenzied seconds search did he discover that the runner's heart was on the right side. (1967)

The only really useful thing about ageing is you can legitimately forget everybody's name," Eric Idle, whose musical *Spamalot* has just opened in America, tells *Men's Health*. "Only the other day at some function I asked a grey-haired chap with piggy eyes what he was doing these days. 'I'm still President,' he said." (2005)

• • •

We were intrigued to hear this week about the beginnings of rose hip syrup, nowadays essential drinking for any baby with aspirations to bonniness. Mr AW Kay, chairman of the National Rose Hip Products Association, says that the first juice was extracted at Long Ashton Research Station by a professor who crushed the hips by running over them with the station's lawn roller weighted with the professor's secretary. But, says Mr Kay, the ministry of health were not amused when they received the report "satisfactory extraction achieved by exerting pressure equal to one lawn roller plus one secretary ". Later, the method was refined by using a motorised domestic mangle. Today the industry uses 600 tons of hips a year and employs 60,000 people, largely schoolchildren, gipsies and members of women's institutes. (1966)

• • •

You don't have to be touched to serve in Mrs Thatcher's Cabinet but it obviously helps. A Cabinet minister recently boarded a London-bound train after a speech in Liverpool, only to find carriage after carriage offering nothing but standing room. Eventually he found an empty compartment labelled "Reserved for Runcorn Mental Hospital" and took a seat. Shortly after, a group of patients boarded and seated themselves around him, whereupon the accompanying nurse started to count his charges. After he got to three he spotted the interloper and demanded to know his identity. The seat-stealer owned up to being John Wakeham, the secretary of state for energy. "Four," continued the nurse without pause, "five, six…" (1990)

• • •

A pamphlet published by the department of health and social security about the new regional health authorities (RHAs) gives details of proposed community health councils. It reports: "Two thirds of the members will be appointed by local authorities, one third by voluntary bodies and the remainder by the RHA." The RHAs should read the small print before agreeing. (1974)

"Albert's determined to become the first 100mph bowler"

SPORT

At a dinner for the publication of the new *Wisden Cricketers' Almanack*, I heard that the publishers were asked to give permission for a racehorse to be named after the reference book. Wisden, a two-year-old colt, was bought by John Warren, the Queen's bloodstock adviser, for the Highclere racing syndicate, but the horse was a bit too frisky in the stables and has been gelded. It's another no-balls scandal for English cricket. (2015)

· · ·

It's still an affluent society. A colleague, driving through a run-down area of Southwark, saw a group of teenagers putting a blank wall on a council estate to good use – practising their golf drives. (1980)

· · ·

Jamie Roberts, the Wales rugby player, was the guest speaker at Guildhall in London for a St David's Day bash. Roberts, who is training to be a surgeon, said that some of his team-mates were not particularly bright. He once shared a room with Mike Phillips, the scrum half, who asked about a blemish on Roberts's backside. "That's a birth mark," Roberts said. "Oh," Phillips replied. "How long have you had that?" (2016)

· · ·

Lee Byrne, the former Wales full back, complained at the same dinner that his countrymen didn't get treated the same as their England counterparts. "All the former English players end up getting gongs," he sighed. "I've had an STD, but I want an MBE or a CBE. I'd even settle for a GCSE, to be honest." (2016)

More on the Eton-Harrow cricket match, Lord's oldest fixture. A spectator reports that, for the first time, there were streakers – both of them male. "Too well developed to have been schoolboys," barked my man. "But clearly well brought up – they made sure they avoided the wicket." (1995)

. . .

Trevor Bayliss, England's Ashes-winning coach, was at a dinner with Sir Ian Botham, who was ostentatiously flashing a chunky watch costing tens of thousands of pounds that he said had been given to him as a birthday present by Eric Clapton. "What time does it say?" Bayliss asked. "Quarter to ten," Botham replied. "That's funny," Bayliss said, looking at his own £50 watch. "So does mine." (2015)

. . .

To the Café Royal in London and the Cancer Research UK sporting Turn the Tables fundraiser, at which sports celebrities quiz journalists. Step forward the former England and Tottenham striker Gary Lineker, who was quizzed by the rugby player Gareth Chilcott about footballers' wages. "It is unbelievable, the money they earn now," he said. Of course, in this era of vast wages, poor Gary no longer plays football. He just gets paid £2 million a year by the BBC to talk about it. (2008)

. . .

Sir Peter O'Sullevan, the racing commentator who died this week, would never let something like a bomb scare get in the way of work. When the Grand National had to be evacuated in 1997, he insisted on returning to the commentary box. "The captain should be on the bridge," he said. It took three policemen to stop him. As they dragged him away from Aintree, he offered a wager. "£100 it's a hoax," he declared. "If we live, you pay. If we get blown to bits, I'll owe you." (2015)

• • •

Pity the England rugby team, forced to attend a reception at Buckingham Palace last night after being knocked out of their own World Cup. Let's hope that Prince George, whose father cheered for Wales when they beat England, wasn't toddling around in a red outfit. Many years ago the England team were introduced to Princess Anne and her children before they played Scotland. Peter Phillips, who was then about 12, suddenly grimaced and started to weep on meeting Wade Dooley, the England lock. "What happened there?" Paul Ackford, Dooley's second-row partner, asked. "The little bastard was wearing a Scotland shirt," Dooley replied. "So I crushed his hand." (2015)

• • •

If Manchester can bid for the Olympics why can the Ryder Cup not come to Hampstead Heath? It may sound foolish but the comic Peter Cook is today putting forward a proposal to bring Nick Faldo and the rest to the heath in 2001. Cook has formed a Hampstead Heath Ryder Cup Committee and is planning at least one innovation. "There is to be random drug testing," he says. "If the committee finds anything good they get to keep it." (1993)

• • •

Paul Stonehouse sent in a photo from Liverpool John Lennon airport, whose slogan is "above us only sky". Someone had added: "Below us only QPR and Reading." (2015)

Sir Matthew Pinsent decided to have a serious talk with his three children about his plans in the event of anything happening to him and his wife. The oarsman-turned-presenter, winner of four Olympic gold medals, discussed wills, guardians, inheritance, etc, only for one of his sons to pipe up: "Who gets your torch?" Well, you can't blame a child for wanting a piece of memorabilia, especially when his dad is one of our greatest Olympians, but it turns out he wasn't referring to the gold flaming torch that Pinsent had carried in the London 2012 relay. "No, it was just a standard battery-driven number powered by three AAAs," Pinsent says. "And none of them had any concern for my medals." (2014)

· · ·

Kristin Scott Thomas cannot decide, as a Brit living in Paris, who should host the 2012 Olympics. "I would rather run 1,000 miles to avoid either city having to host the Olympics," she said. "That's an idea for an alternative Olympic sport – a race between right-minded people trying to flee the awful thing." (2005)

· · ·

The spirit of Evelyn Waugh's *Scoop* lives on. Those who fondly remember William Boot, the nature columnist in Waugh's novel who is accidentally sent to a war zone, will delight in a tale sent to me by a colleague in the Middle East who was on a bus travelling to an Asian Cup football match in Beirut when he heard a *Daily Telegraph* sports correspondent shouting into his mobile phone (presumably into his news desk). "It's fine," he yelled. "It's lovely, the sun's shining. I'm walking around in shorts and a T-shirt." There was a pause and then:

"Oh. That climate. Um, there's been no trouble but I think the Palestinians are planning some sort of march today." (2000)

. . .

The Hong Kong rugby sevens is a great *Gweilo* shindig – *Gweilo* means ghost person and is the Cantonese term for a European. To the colony's five million Cantonese, rugby is a complete mystery. The Chinese have never been encouraged to play the game in Hong Kong, though elsewhere they have taken to it: the sevens include a team from Taiwan and the Singapore team will have four Chinese. But this will probably be the total Chinese population in the stadium: the Hong Kong Chinese will have more important things to do today, like racing at Happy Valley. This is a sport the Hong Kong Chinese love to distraction. There are eight races today, with such auspiciously named beasts as Constant Win, Money Maker, Money Flavour and Silver Abacus duelling for mastery. On Wednesday, one of the runners was bizarrely named Mediocre. It came second. It must be hard to shout "Come on Mediocre". (1988)

. . .

Sir Stanley Rous, president of the International Football Association, has discovered a simply splendid weapon with which to wage the great but deadly game of Lifemanship. At Wimbledon, for example, he turned up among the royal party at Centre Court looking more than usually inscrutable behind a pair of heavy dark glasses and astonished members of the All-England Club by his omniscience about events on the other courts. The secret lay in his dark glasses. They concealed a small transistor radio relayed through what looks like a deaf aid: "I didn't half get some funny looks," he recalls. "Obviously people were thinking 'not only is the old boy deaf, but he believes he's got second sight'." (1967)

"I'm just going to spend a euro"

EUROPE

Last Friday's issue of *Hansard* contained one of those priceless typographical errors which occur only rarely in this outstandingly accurate publication. It reports Reginald Freeson, minister for housing and construction, as saying: "Tonight we are concerned with a daft EEC directive on…" Well, they say you can't gag *Hansard* and there has been many a time when MPs have complained that some of the draft directives on harmonisation emanating from the European Commission are little else but daft. (1977)

• • •

Helmut Schmidt died yesterday, having reached 96 despite a huge tobacco habit. It was once estimated that the German chancellor had a cigarette every seven minutes. In 2013, the EU proposed a ban on his favourite menthol cigarettes, so Schmidt is said to have stockpiled 38,000 of them, which it was thought would keep him going for two years. Maybe that's why he died: he finally ran out of puff. (2015)

• • •

The European Parliament's output of paper uses 80 trees a month to produce a pile of bumf 28 times the height of Nelson's Column. During one five-day meeting in Strasbourg in October 1980, Euro-MPs used 5,770,880 pages of documents. The total for the month was 12,619,685 pages. The parliament's departments are currently translating 250,000 pages a year into seven languages and printing more than 100 million pages. The 434 members of the European Parliament receive each document on average five or six times, at their various homes and offices. At this rate the parliament will have laid waste a forest of 4,800 trees by the next election. The report from which these facts are drawn is itself 22 pages long. (1982)

The BBC Overseas Service in its European English programme recently mounted a competition for its Continental listeners with the theme "The British: are they Europeans ?" The response so far includes entries from every European country except Albania and some of them make entertaining reading. There is the man from Malaga who argues that the British are not Europeans because they "have a mother country, others have a fatherland. Women became the British destiny from Boadicea to Mrs Castle[29]". A listener in Johanneshov, Sweden, disagrees. The British race, he argues, includes Gaelic, Roman and German strains. "It is difficult to find anything so European in the rest of Europe ." (1967)

• • •

An invitation to a meeting in Southend contains the following directions: "On leaving the station turn right down the High Street and walk in the general direction of France." It will be interesting to see how many make it. (1980)

• • •

It was a satisfied, even proud, John Uding who returned to Amsterdam airport from London. It is not every day that a man is elected president of the Confederation of European Pest Control Associations. The glow of satisfaction dimmed and went out when he got into his parked car. It was infested with mice. Chocolate had been nibbled and papers chewed up to make a nest. Even their map of Amsterdam had been eroded, in place of the location of his company's offices in the city there was now a jagged hole. Mr Uding, head of the Rentokil company in The Netherlands, has not entirely ruled out revenge as the motive. (1977)

---

[29] Barbara Castle, at the time the transport secretary.

John Marshall, Tory MP for North London, is seeking to bowl a googly to the council of ministers next week when he will ask them to propose "that the knowledge of cricket be spread throughout the [European] Community". Marshall, a Middlesex supporter, believes that cricket "teaches you not to change the rules halfway through the game". This is what he believes the Community did last month in depriving Britain of its right to veto agricultural prices. The council has spotted his disguised off break. When he asks the question next week in Strasbourg he will politely be told "No", which is called keeping a straight bat. (1982)

• • •

Margaret Thatcher, minister of education, is taking French lessons. The assumption is that she wants to be minister for Europe. (1973)

• • •

Geography lessons are in order for Chris Smith, the shadow health secretary, who grew horribly confused when buying the stamps for his Christmas cards in the House of Commons post office the other day. He was told by the clerk that there were three rates for foreign mail: one for the world except Europe, one for the EU and one for European countries outside the EU. Smith riffled through his cards, then asked: "Is Israel in Europe?" Although it competes in the Eurovision Song Contest, he was told, it is not in Europe. "What about Switzerland," he then said, "is that in the EU?" (1996)

Conservative Central Office is issuing T-shirts emblazoned with the party slogan: Put Britain First. They were made in Portgual. (1974)

• • •

Life and Work, the record of the Church of Scotland, commissioned a Prayer for Europe from the Holy Tryst Committee. The result is worthy of that great Scottish verse-maker, William McGonagall. Here is the first verse:

> Our God,
> We are now in the Common Market
> Some of us feel this has been a mistake,
> Some of us believe this will bring opportunities for good,
> Most of us just don't know. (1973)

• • •

Our prime minister is going to the Elysee from the embassy this morning by car. For a healthy chap like Edward Heath, this is a little odd: the distance is no more than 200 yards. But protocol demands it, he could not just wander in. The trouble is that the Rue du Foubourg St Honore, in which the Elysee and the embassy stand, is a one-way street in the wrong direction. So either Heath has to be driven by way of the American embassy and the Elysee's back door, or else all the traffic is stopped and vast traffic jams are allowed while the embassy Rolls drives the wrong way up the street. This is what was done for Harold Wilson in 1967, as a token of esteem, and it did irreparable harm to Anglo-French relations among a small but noisy cross-section of Parisian motorists. (1971)

"Unfortunately, lions are not bound by the Geneva Convention."

LIBERALS AND OTHER PARTY ANIMALS

Andrew Neil bumped into Baroness Williams of Crosby at the Lib Dems' conference after he had finished presenting *Daily Politics* on BBC Two. "I've just been toasting your leader," the broadcaster said. "Oh, how nice of you," replied a tickled Shirley. "Not with champagne," corrected Neil. "I've been sticking his feet in the fire in an interview." Must have been quite a grilling. (2009)

• • •

Ronnie Carroll picked up 113 votes in Hampstead & Kilburn at the general election despite the disadvantage of having died during the campaign. This is 84 more votes than Carroll, a former British entry for the Eurovision Song Contest, got when he stood as a living and breathing candidate in a parliamentary by-election in 2008. (2015)

• • •

Screaming Lord Sutch[30] did not lose his deposit in the Darlington by-election. He forfeited his £150, of course, but won it back by betting £50 at 3 to 1 with William Hill that he would poll more than 250 votes. In the event he got 374, and came fourth, a marked improvement on Bermondsey where he finished sixth with only 97. A psephologist writes: If this pattern was repeated all over the country and the swing could be maintained in election after election, Screaming Lord Sutch would become prime minister some time in the middle of the next century. (1983)

---

[30] A former musician who founded the Monster Raving Loony Party and led it from 1983 until his death in 1999.

A reader who used to work with Nigel Farage's father emails with a story that explains where the Ukip leader's odd sense of humour came from. Farage Sr, who pronounced the surname "farridge", liked to liven up quiet afternoons in the office by telephoning the Cavalry Club. When the receptionist answered, he would yell "CHARGE!" and hang up. (2014)

• • •

Several reporters have been disappointed at the bar of the Grand Hotel in Brighton in their search for some more of the champagne they enjoyed during the TUC conference last week. The barmen explained that they had not laid on fresh stocks, because from experience they did not think the Liberals could afford it. (1974)

• • •

The Ukip party in South Thanet, where Nigel Farage is standing at the general election, took the BBC's *Daily Politics* to task for filming largely negative vox pops about their leader "in front of a mosque", saying it was a selective location for a supposedly random poll. What a pity that they didn't recognise the neo-Byzantine building with a campanile as Westminster Cathedral, seat of England's Catholics for more than a century. (2014)

• • •

"I've been speaking for an hour and I don't see why I should be giving these interviews to small, unimportant newspapers." Thus began David Owen's pre-arranged chat with a student newspaper after he had addressed the Bristol University Union last week. "I was flabbergasted", says the paper's editor, Susanna Voyle. "He had just spent ten minutes of his speech complaining about poor media coverage of the SDP." (1985)

• • •

Nigel Farage was in a Brechtian mood during Thursday's debate, blaming the lack of applause for him on an audience that was left-wing even for the BBC. Perhaps if he fares badly in the election he'll blame it on the wrong kind of voters. Bertolt Brecht, the Marxist playwright, once wrote that it would be "simpler for the government to dissolve the people and elect another".

Farage was grumpy because someone had swiped his gin. The Ukip leader had asked for a bottle to be placed in his dressing-room, but a puritan jobsworth at the Methodist Central Hall (the clue is in the name) had it removed. Thus deprived of booze, Farage had to content himself with jeers. (2015)

• • •

While David Steel was preparing to first-foot it round his Borders village at Hogmanay, he was also trying to work out details of the new Alliance party's policy declaration with SDP leader Bob Maclennan, who was in America. With the Liberal leader due to set off for Kenya as Maclennan returned to London, the two were communicating by fax. But talk was halted at one point when "Bob from Boston" (as he became known in the Steel household) phoned to talk about a document he had just transmitted. Steel, not known for his technological competence, looked in vain for the article – until he realized he had plugged in the iron instead of the fax machine. (1988)

Charles Kennedy had many talents, but fashion was not one. A story was told at a memorial service for the former Lib Dem leader yesterday of how he quickly came to Margaret Thatcher's attention after being elected in 1983. "Who is that?" she asked Michael Forsyth. That, Forsyth replied, is the SDP member who took your energy minister's seat. An aghast Thatcher replied: "Are you telling me that Hamish Gray was defeated by a man who wears white socks?" (2015)

• • •

Sometimes, the home office issues fictional passports. Did you know that? We didn't. For reasons best known to himself, Nick Clegg (Lib Dem, home affairs) extracted this information from John Reid, the home secretary. It seems that four fictional passports have been issued since 2000. Alarmingly, the whereabouts of one of these remains unknown. James Bond's *Casino Royale* passport is still in use, and those issued to Thomas Sweeney (of *Brookside*) and Diana Begley (of *Blue Murder*) have been destroyed. The passport issued to one Columbus Bear has, however, utterly disappeared. Happily, for border security, Columbus Bear is a bear. (2007)

• • •

Channel 4 is making a film on the birth of the coalition, dubbed *Clegg: The Movie*. Yet such a film already exists. Simon Mason points us to *Clegg*, a forgotten 1969 Brit-flick. It seems to be a low budget version of *Get Carter*, where the hero spends half the film being beaten up and half not receiving any cash from his partners. So very much like being leader of the Lib Dems. (2014)

The odour of Paddy Ashdown is damaging business in an Oxfordshire pub. The Booty Inn invited Ashdown to send some footwear to join a collection that includes cast-offs from Sir Ranulph Fiennes and Stirling Moss. A pair of filthy mud-encrusted plimsolls arrived for the pub's dining-room with an apologetic note from the Lib Dem leader. "I hope they are not too ripe for your diners," it said. "As you can probably tell, they have served me well on many a run over Somerset's beautiful hills." Oh yes. After being placed between Fiennes' mountain boots and Yasmin Le Bon's slingbacks, the management is taking action. "Customers complain bitterly about the smell," says John Flint, publican. "They insist we move them. They are putting them off their dinner." (1998)

. . .

Even allowing that he is a Liberal Democrat (and this particular Lib Dem, to boot) there was a startling lack of dignity to Lembit Opik's opening line at PMQs. "Not wishing to be cheeky, Mr Speaker," he began. "I thank the House of being so happy that I am so very, very lucky! And I should point out that the other sister is still single!" Amid merry guffaws, he then went on to ask a question about motor neurone disease.[31] (2007)

. . .

Westminster was buzzing with cracks and cheap jibes during the defence debate yesterday when the Liberal defence spokesman, Paddy Ashdown, took the floor bearing a spectacular black eye. The former Special Boat Squadron commando, it emerged, was thumped on

[31] Opik, the MP for Montgomeryshire from 1997-2010, was a relentless self-publicist. At the time of this story, he had started dating one of the Cheeky Girls, a Romanian pop act, who was 18 years his junior.

Tuesday night when he disturbed a man tampering with a car parked in Kennington, London. Ashdown, who had been working late on his defence speech, tells me he rang the police when he became suspicious but, fearing it would be too late, "had a go". The incident will amuse John Hume, SDLP member for Foyle. As a civil rights activist, he suffered the humiliation of being arrested at a Londonderry riot by Ashdown, then serving with the Royal Marines in Northern Ireland. Yesterday Ashdown insisted he doesn't make a habit of nabbing folk: "My hobby's winemaking. I'm a gentle soul really." (1985)

*Despite some initial misgivings,
the White House doctor gave
the President-elect a clean
bill of health.*

AMERICANS

Ed Miliband left his debate crib sheet in a bin last week, which *The Sun* has gleefully reproduced. It could have been worse. In 2010, Sarah Palin, the American politician of negligible intellect, was caught looking down at her hands where she had written key phrases in ink. One of them was "lift American spirits", which may have inspired the members of her family who were involved in an alcohol-fuelled brawl at a snowmobile party last year. George W Bush was also advised to write notes on the back of his hands in case he should forget the basics during a debate. The joke went that on his left hand he wrote "breathe in" and on his right "breathe out". (2015)

. . .

Fortnum and Mason has these days not only its clock figures representing the founding partners emerging to strike the hour, but two employees dressed as Mr F. and Mr M. who perambulate through its thickly carpeted departments. An American customer who entered the store the other day to be confronted by Fortnum was clearly startled. "Gee," she told him, "you got down mighty quick from that clock outside, didn't you?" (1968)

. . .

Martin Rees, the astronomer royal, gave a speech at Harvard last month in which he warned that mankind was sowing the seeds of its destruction. He touched on this in a book a few years back that he had wanted to be called *Our Final Century?*, but his publisher deleted the question mark, since certainty sells better. His American publisher then changed the title to *Our Final Hour*. "Americans seek instant gratification," Lord Rees explained. (2014)

American television news programme – which are sprinkled with advertisements – are notoriously prone to lapses of taste. On Sunday night a shampoo advertisement interrupted the CBS 11 o'clock news. From jingle singer to sombre announcer, the programme went thus:

"You've got body with Halo. Halo's got body to give."

"In Washington today the body of General Dwight D. Eisenhower was conveyed in State . . .

This is perhaps the worst gaffe of its kind since April 1965, when the announcement of Ed Murrow's death and the fact that he had died of lung cancer were separated by an advertisement offering "longer lasting smoking pleasure". (1969)

• • •

Matthew Barzun, the engaging American ambassador, has gradually learnt to adapt to British life after 18 months here, even if he had a slight grumble a while ago about the food. His wife, however, has found the transition much harder. "I struggle with the fashion vocabulary," Brooke Barzun said at an awards gala at Goldsmiths' Hall in the City. "Adjusting to 'jumper' instead of 'sweater' was hard, but my casual reference to 'pants' rather than 'trousers' yielded me some strange looks." It was bum bags, though, that really caused a problem for Barzun, who said: "In the interest of diplomacy I would rather not go into the harrowing ordeal of searching online to get my children 'fanny packs'." (2015)

Students and faculty at Brigham Young University in Utah have united to protest about a planned appearance by Vice-President Dick Cheney. In terms of personal integrity, "Cheney just doesn't measure up," said one professor at the university, which was named after a Mormon who had 52 wives and 57 known children. (2007)

• • •

A year after Bill Clinton left the White House and just after she had become a US senator, Hillary Clinton returned to Yale, where she read law, to give the benefit of her advice about politics. "This may be the most important thing I say to you," she announced. "Hair matters. Pay attention to your hair, because everyone else will."

That same year, the man who may be Hillary's biggest block on the path back to the White House proved that very point. If there is one thing that Donald Trump feels sensitive about, it is his ridiculous combed-over hairdo. So much so that when a friend wrote in another British paper in 2001 that Trump had "hair by Bobby Charlton and a Homer Simpson stomach", he was surprised to get a phone call from Trump Towers itself. "Saywhaddyaplayinat?" Trump shouted down the line at him, before adding: "And who the hell is Bob Charleston anyway? Some sort of limey barber?" (2015)

• • •

A London tour guide, addressing a group of American tourists somewhere near Holborn: "...and that, ladies and gentlemen, is the London School of Economics, otherwise known as the LSE, where students include your very own Monica Lewinsky. I do believe she has recently done very well in her orals." Long pause. "Which are what we call spoken exams".[32] (2006)

---

[32] Lewinsky became infamous in 1998 when news broke that she had given oral sex to Bill Clinton in the Oval Office while working as a White House intern.

Such is the mass of information that has come our way concerning Charlton Heston (gun lover, ape nemesis), who died on Saturday, that we hereby begin a temporary regular slot entitled: Things We Can't Believe We Didn't Know About Charlton Heston. So, today's nugget concerns the Waco siege of 1993, during which, we learn, Heston was approached by the FBI. This was part of a swiftly abandoned plan in which he was to pretend to be God, and they were to transmit his voice to cult leader David Koresh. Seriously. (2008)

• • •

Word from the set of the US reality series *The Apprentice* is that Donald Trump is ready to do his bit for racial and ethnic understanding. He wants to pit a team of black people against a team of white people. "Whether people like it or not, it is somewhat reflective of our very vicious world," Trump said. (2005)

• • •

A little vignette of American sporting life. A man named Michael Clark, of Fairfield, Virginia, got rather upset at a baseball match the other day. The object of his ire was, as one might expect, the umpire, Steve Rohr. Rohr gave a batter out for the crime of stepping out of the batter's box. Clark allegedly attacked the umpire and police say that when he was ejected from the field, he produced a gun – a .357 magnum, to be pedantic. He has been charged with assault. You might think such things are usual at American sporting events – but not, surely, at a game between teams of girls aged between eight and 11. (1988)

Jerry Springer[33], in London to speak at a dinner for the United Jewish Israel Appeal, defended his show's guests against transatlantic sneers. "Maybe they aren't as rich as other people, maybe they don't speak the Queen's English, but let's be honest – there are some pretty powerful and wealthy people over here in England who could very well be guests on my show. You just give them titles." (2005)

. . .

From the *Washington Post* came entries for The Worst Analogies Ever Written in a High School Essay contest: "The little boat drifted across the pond exactly the way a bowling ball wouldn't"; "He was as tall as a six-foot three-inch tree." And one I don't think is so bad: "The hailstones leaped from the pavement, just like maggots when you fry them in hot grease." (1996)

. . .

When the Americans were building their new embassy they were anxious that their flag-pole should outreach all others. So the ambassador phoned his British counterpart with an innocent-sounding query about the exact height of his pole. The British ambassador immediately gave him the answer, but when the American pole was built it was still a few feet shorter than ours. The wily and perfidious Briton, well taught in the cunning ways of diplomacy, had instantly recognised the motive of the American's question. So he had lied by a crucial dozen feet or so. Our ambassadors are wonderful. (1974)

---

[33] Host of an American tabloid talk show, in which guests would air their family grievances and often come to blows.

In a characteristically bracing way, Canada's prime minister Pierre Trudeau has been telling crowds in New Brunswick, where he has been on a brisk tour, that he spent Ascension Day going up in a Voodoo jet. It seems that he took over the controls and reached "bravo" (jargon for the sound barrier) 75 miles out over the St Lawrence Gulf. On his return the station commander, worried about defence cuts, asked Trudeau: "Do you think it's here to last?" The Prime Minister is said to have replied: "Do you mean flying? It will probably last as long as sex." (1969)

• • •

An ex-Harvard reader was interested by my revelation last week that Dr Kissinger[34] really was the model for Dr Strangelove in the film. He attended a course in international government relations given by Kissinger in the late 1950s and recalls that Kissinger opened the course by saying in a thick German accent: "At the end of the Second World War we should have imposed our domination over the whole world. We had the strength and we had the means but we lacked the determination." After some minutes' stunned silence, Kissinger added: "We, Americans." (1973)

• • •

Hillary Clinton has an impressive CV but she has never handed Middlesbrough an away trip to Peterborough United. Her likely rival for the White House has. Donald Trump bizarrely appeared on the ITV football show *Saint & Greavsie* in 1992 and helped with the draw for the quarter-finals of the League Cup. "Peter-bow-row?" Trump asked.

---

[34] German-born US secretary of state under Richard Nixon and Gerald Ford. *Dr Strangelove* was a 1964 black comedy film that satirised the Cold War and the threat of nuclear attack.

"Are they a good team?" Jimmy Greaves assured him that they were one of the best. The former England player then gave Trump a *Saint & Greavsie* mug. "The most prestigious cup in football," he said, showing how, if you poured hot coffee into it, the slogan "It's a funny old game" glowed on the side. I wonder if Trump still has it. (2016)

*"And remember, chaps, you'll be
going to Shell and back"*

FOREIGN POLICY

It's a wonderful thing, government intelligence. "I had the rather dubious honour of being the highest-level American official to meet with Kim Jong Il," said Madeline Albright, Bill Clinton's ever-diplomatic secretary of state, at her book launch this week. "We didn't know a lot about him. Our intelligence said that he was crazy and a pervert. He's not crazy." (2006)

. . .

A group of leading Labour MPs have just returned from an official trip to China, which they found curiously hierarchical for a supposedly communist country. They travelled in a cavalcade of cars. John Smith, the shadow chancellor, went first in a Mercedes. He was followed by George Foulkes (foreign affairs), Mark Fisher (arts), Tony Blair[35] (trade and industry) and the former Labour MP Laurie Pavitt, each in Japanese cars whose descending order of engine power directly reflected their seniority. (1988)

. . .

Over lunch with Lord Rothschild at Spencer House yesterday, the Israeli foreign secretary, Shimon Peres, was ruminating about the chances of a peace treaty with Syria. He at least credits President Assad of Syria with a sense of humour. Assad recently told him: "I can't understand why everyone says I'm surrounded by yes-men. Whenever I say 'no' all the people around me say 'no' too!" (1995)

---

[35] This was the first mention of the future Labour prime minister in the Diary.

Lord Howell of Guildford revealed in a debate this week a conversation he once had with Valéry Giscard D'Estaing, the president of France. "He told me that at school he was taught that the Battle of Trafalgar was a minor naval engagement in which the British were stupid enough to lose their admiral." (2015)

• • •

It was with some triumph that the newly appointed Robin Cook announced that he would remove a portrait of General Ranajee, commander-in-chief of Nepal at the height of empire, from his foreign office study. Instead, he wanted something that would reflect Britain's hip new future. At last, our smooth-operating foreign secretary has found a suitable replacement: a vast mirror, in which our dashing friend can admire the living embodiment of Cool Britannia. (1998)

• • •

Because last week's Labour Party conference was held in the cramped Central Hall at Westminster, there were insufficient places for all the overseas observers who wanted to attend. Assigning tickets was a perilous business. In the initial assignment there was no ticket for the representative of tiny Guyana. So anxious was he to attend, however, that he telephoned Transport House and delivered dire threats about what might happen to Britain's sugar supplies from his country if he did not get in. A ticket was therefore found for him with some dispatch by sweet-toothed party functionaries. The representative of oil-rich Bahrain was allocated a ticket without having to threaten anything. (1974)

More on Oliver Miles, the former ambassador to Libya who was the principal author of the letter to the prime minister by the diplomats attacking his policies on the Middle East.

When he was ambassador to Luxembourg in the 1980s, Margaret Thatcher, then prime minister, stayed overnight in his residence. Over breakfast his children bravely took issue with Thatcher over Nelson Mandela. They chorused: "Why don't you stop supporting apartheid in South Africa?" The Iron Lady replied: "Why don't you go to school?" (2004)

• • •

Neil Kinnock is revealing a talent for excruciating puns in Franglais. Told about the hijack of the lorry drivers and their cargo of British lamb just before his visit to Paris last week, the Labour leader remarked, "It's viande a joke". I hope he forgot to tell that one to President Meaterrand. (1984)

• • •

A Nigerian transport company inserted this plaintive announcement in the *Daily Times* of Lagos: "Our unhealthy competitors and their touts are engaged in carrying about false and unfounded rumours in order to attract our customers. We wish to state categorically to the general public and our customers that none of our numerous drivers was ever swallowed by a boa constrictor in a bush near Ore Town. The rumours should be regarded as false and unpatriotic." (1976)

The French never lose their sense of chic, not even at the security check at Charles de Gaulle airport, Paris. A colleague watched a woman passenger present herself for weapon screening, wearing a jaunty hat held at its angle by a huge and potentially lethal hatpin, which was regarded suspiciously by the guards. "Mais vous comprenez", she murmured sweetly, "pour le chapeau il fait absolutment..." She was whisked through with adoring smiles of understanding, fully equipped to open whelks or stab the entire cabin crew in the back. (1981)

• • •

The funeral of Yuri Andropov today prompts my colleague Gabriel Ronay to recall an evening he spent downing vodkas with Andropov in Budapest in 1956. Working as a Hungarian interpreter for a Soviet cultural delegation, Ronay attended a reception hosted by Andropov, then Soviet ambassador in Budapest. Since the Russian visitors were led by a senior Central Committee member, Andropov felt it necessary to embark on an extensive round of toasts, featuring virtually everyone in the Kremlin leadership from Khrushchev down. Ronay, alarmed at the prospect at getting too drunk to interpret, arranged with a waiter to have his glass refilled each time with tap water. Imagine his embarrassment, after it was all over, when Andropov remarked that the product of Budapest's taps hardly compared with Russian's own fiery water. Clearly the ambassador understood Hungarian. Then it occurred to Ronay that, since Andropov was the only other sober person present, he must also have made a diplomatic arrangement with the waiter. (1984)

Clement Freud likes to tell of a visit to China earlier this year as a member of a parliamentary delegation, which also included Winston Churchill. At the end Freud said to his Chinese hosts: "I know you never do anything without reason, so why is it Mr Churchill was given a better hotel room that mine?" The answer came back: "Well, Mr Churchill had a very famous grandfather" to which the grandson of psychoanalyst Sigmund Freud had absolutely no reply. (1986)

• • •

Lord Bethell has an ingenious explanation gleaned from a Czechoslovak friend visiting London for Russian troops' slowness in leaving that country. In the Bratislavan district, this friend reports, fraternisation between Soviet soldiery and the local population had thriven. In particular the poorly paid Russians were subsidising their visits to Bratislavan bars and high-spots by the sale of petrol illicitly syphoned from army vehicles. The inference is plain: the Russian army could not move because it was low on petrol and high on vodka. (1968)

• • •

There is still some rigidity in the uppers lips in our foreign embassies, if our diplomats continue to adopt the attitude taken by Sir John Whitehead, Britain's ambassador to Japan a decade ago. Lord Lang of Monkton, a Cabinet minister under John Major, recalls in his memoirs a visit to the ambassador's residence in Tokyo. Suddenly, the chandeliers started tinkling, the walls shook and a terrified Lang realised he was in the middle of an earthquake. He was still in a state of nervous fretfulness when Lady Whitehead strode into the room. "These earthquakes are such a bore," she said. "One has to go round the house afterwards, straightening all the pictures." (2002)

Press officers accompanying foreign secretaries in overseas tours are often required to act above and beyond the call of duty, but none more so than Andrew Burns, 46, who stands down today as head of the foreign office press corps. Burns's colleagues still recall with admiration the occasion when he accompanied a party of journalists on a river voyage in Djibouti in the Horn of Africa. He was on the last leg of Sir Geoffrey Howe's Middle East tour and the boat started to sink. An admirer recalls: "Burns simply took off his shoe and bailed until they reached dry land." The foreign office was last night too busy fêting Burns on his departure to confirm his shoe size. (1990)

• • •

I should not wish to end without offering my congratulations to President Ceausescu on becoming Hero of Romania, his country's highest honour, which he has just awarded to himself. No braver man ever deserved the title: my sources in Bucharest tell me that his attempt to kiss himself on both cheeks was prevented only on the intervention of his osteopath. (1988)

• • •

The British parliamentary group that recently visited Moscow spent much of its time wondering why Lord Whitelaw, its leader, was receiving such exaggerated deference from his Soviet hosts. The explanation turned out to be *Pravda*'s translation of Whitelaw's official title: Lord President of the Privy Council. This had somehow turned out as "Secret Council", which was enough to convince the Russians that they were being visited by the head of MI5. (1986)

Senior officials in the foreign and commonwealth office and the ministry of defence are now regretting Sir Alec Douglas-Home's action in expelling 105 Soviet diplomats earlier this year. The Russian embassy has retaliated by stopping traditional seasonal gifts of vodka, caviar and candy. (1971)

BARRY FANTONI

'Anything you say will be taken
down and used in my memoirs'

BOOKS AND AUTHORS

The Ecuadorean embassy could soon get its ladies' bathroom back with the suggestion that Julian Assange is about to leave[36]. When he was under "manor arrest" at Ellingham Hall in Norfolk in 2011, he told a would-be ghostwriter, Andrew O'Hagan, that he planned to convert a stable into his office. "A book was born in a manger," Assange said with customary humility. The Messiah was deflated when O'Hagan pointed out he'd never find three wise men in Norfolk, never mind a virgin. (2014)

· · ·

Ion Trewin, who wrote this column from 1969-72, has died. He ran the Booker Prize, but was best known for publishing Alan Clark's diaries.[37] To secure the contract, he not only took along a sample of the creamy, thick paper he wanted to use — which Clark found "sensual" — but brought Caroline Michel, a new member of his marketing team, now a literary agent. "Caroline put her job first," Trewin wrote. "Knowing Clark's propensities, she wore a tiny miniskirt." Whatever it takes … (2015)

· · ·

A reader thinks I may not have seen the graffiti in the gentlemen's lavatory at Cambridge University Library. Quite right. Here it is:

> To do is to be – JS Mill.
> And underneath, in another hand:
> To be is to do – Jean-Paul Sartre.
> Rounded out by a third hand:
> Do be do be do – Frank Sinatra. (1973)

---

[36] Assange, an Australian computer programmer and founder of WikiLeaks, which publishes leaked classified information, took refuge in Ecuador's London embassy in 2012 to avoid extradition to Sweden to face questioning about rape allegations.

[37] The racy, indiscreet and highly entertaining diaries of the former Tory defence minister.

For our series on mistranslations, Maria Mosby recalls a tale from Elaine Steinbeck, widow of John Steinbeck, author of *The Grapes of Wrath*. She was taken aback in Japan when asking the clerk in a Yokohama bookshop if they had any books by her husband. "Yes," came the reply. "We have The Angry Raisins." (2015)

• • •

My favourite taxi story, told in a letter to *The Times* by the subject's widow in 1970, involves a poet getting into a cab. "You're TS Eliot," the driver informed him. When asked how he knew, he replied: "Ah, I've got an eye for a celebrity. Only the other evening I picked up Bertrand Russell, and I said to him: 'Well, Lord Russell, what's it all about?' And, do you know, he couldn't tell me." (2015)

• • •

Lord Clark, the art historian, thinks the least welcoming bookshops are in Paris and the most sympathetic are in Britain's provincial towns. His main complaint about London's bookshops is that few of them are designed for browsers. He made these points yesterday when he opened the Antiquarian Book Fair at the Europa Hotel, London. I browsed in a non-antiquarian Fleet Street bookshop yesterday and saw a sign in the window that said: "Wanted, assistant with good sense of humour." Why that qualification? I asked the lady in charge. "You need a sense of humour to work for the wages you get here," she said. (1978)

In a brief revival of our headline series, we've spotted more evidence that Enid Blyton's characters became rather less wholesome on reaching adulthood, with one southwest newspaper revealing: "Five fall victim to revenge porn in Dorset". (2015)

. . .

Faber and Faber held a cosy little party at the National Book League to celebrate the opening of an exhibition marking 50 years of Faber publishing. Lady Faber, wife of the firm's founder, was the senior guest, and many members of the Faber dynasty were present. Faber publishing began with Faber and Gwyer in 1925, becoming Faber and Faber in 1929. The firm has published most of the eminent names in modern English literature – Eliot, Auden, MacNeice, Spender, Osborne, Golding, Durrell. One thing I did not know about the firm is that there never was a second Faber. Geoffrey Faber called it Faber and Faber because he thought it sounded grander than plain Faber. (1975)

. . .

Mark Ellen, the former editor of *The Word* and ex-bandmate of Tony Blair, was in Foyles bookshop yesterday and claims that one of the shop assistants moaned that he had been told off for his mischievous application of "signed by the author" stickers. "What was the problem?" Ellen asked him. "I'd put them on all our Bibles," came the reply. (2015)

. . .

James Cameron[38], whose autobiography has just been published, tells an amusing story about an incident between him and the censor in Tel Aviv recently while he was covering the war. He submitted his first

---

[38] Author and journalist, primarily for the BBC. Died in 1985.

article to the censor, who read it through without a word and then handed the copy of it back to him rather distastefully, saying: "The sentiments are commonplace, Mr Cameron, and the style is banal, but I have no censorship objections to the article." As Cameron said afterwards, the most annoying part about it is that he felt it was true. (1967)

. . .

Americans are sometimes so plain-speaking they can come across as rude. Alexander McCall Smith, bestselling author of such comic novels as *The No 1 Ladies' Detective Agency* recalls being drawn aside by a reader in a bookshop in Atlanta, during a signing tour across the US. "Don't worry," she told the novelist. "I think you'll do far better posthumously." (2014)

. . .

Snoopy[39], scourge of the Red Baron, has just acquired the ability to speak Welsh. The decision by Cardiff publisher Gwasg y Dref Wen to translate two of the books into the old tongue means that Snoopy can now bark in 23 languages, including Serbo-Croat, Chinese and Latin. In Welsh *That's how it goes, Snoopy* has become *Fei na mae, Snwpi*, and *The Ferocity of Snoopy* is now *Ffyrnigrwydd Snwpi*. The Welshmen maintain it is only natural justice, for according to them America was discovered by Prince Madoc decades before Christopher Columbus was born. (1984)

---

[39] Star of the American comic strip series *Peanuts*.

Ion Trewin, the late Booker Prize big cheese, knew the value of getting the title right. At a memorial service, Ann Widdecombe recalled a disagreement over one of her novels. She wanted to call it *An Act of Reconciliation.* "You can't," Trewin, her publisher, said. "It sounds like an accountancy manual." (2015)

. . .

Sir Edward Cazalet recalled sage advice at the launch of an exhibition in Mayfair celebrating his grandfather, PG Wodehouse. "He always said: 'If you want to find out if an author is any good, read their fourth book. One way or another, the first three are biographical. Most writers can produce three books, but it's the fourth one…'." (2009)

. . .

Joyce Carol Oates, the American novelist, is concerned that the media are not giving enough coverage to the lighter side of death-cult terrorism. "All we hear of Isis is puritanical and punitive," she says. (I'm not joking.) "Is there nothing celebratory and joyous?" It's true: the Raqqa Light Operatic Society's recent production of *The Mikado* was under-reported. I hear there was great competition to play the role of Lord High Executioner. (2015)

. . .

Ian McEwan was at the launch of the Science Museum's Collider exhibition to answer the burning question: What do novelists and physicists have in common? Maybe they both depend on fundamental laws and meticulous research? "I often wonder what theoretical physicists do all day," McEwan mused. "My fantasy is that they're rather like novelists and sit there with their feet on the radiator staring out the window." (2013)

Unpublished authors should not despair. American writer Andre Bernard has assembled a collection of morale-sapping rejection letters sent to writers who subsequently became household names. His book, *Rotten Rejections: A Literary Companion*, includes a scathing rejection of Nabokov's *Lolita*. "Overwhelmingly nauseating, even to an enlightened Freudian," declares the anonymous reader in 1955. "I recommend that it be buried under a stone for a thousand years." And when one of the Duke of Edinburgh's favourite books, *Kon-Tiki*, was submitted by Thor Heyerdahl in 1952, he was told: "The idea of men adrift on a raft does have a certain appeal, but for the most part it is a long, solemn and tedious Pacific voyage." Rudyard Kipling fared no better. "I'm sorry, Mr Kipling," he was told after submitting an unknown manuscript in 1889, "but you just don't know how to use the English language." (1990)

• • •

The novelist Kate Mosse is used to being confused with the model whose name is pronounced the same way. "I'm shorter," she tells *Stylist* magazine, helpfully. Just to add to the mix-ups, Mosse's literary agent in America is called George Lucas. There is always this "sad moment of disappointment", she says, when an American restaurant takes their booking and "two rather shabby 'book people' arrive". (2013)

• • •

Graham Greene's consistent refusal to be seen on television will extend beyond the grave. He has just refused an invitation from Stephen Claypole, news editor of BBC television news, to make a film of his life to be broadcast when he dies. "I would gladly hasten my death rather than write my own obituary," he replied, which leaves Claypole with a problem. Glimpses of Greene on film are scarce indeed. They include views of his back for one old BBC programme, of his hands during an interview for *The South Bank Show*, and of his back again when he took a cameo role in the Truffaut film *Day for Night*. So great is Greene's desire for anonymity that even his brother, Sir Hugh Greene, former director-general of the BBC, could not lure him before the cameras. (*1985*)

· · ·

A savage and witty correspondence between Randolph Churchill and Evelyn Waugh, extending from their wartime friendship in Yugoslavia to Waugh's death in 1966, is now to be published. In preparing it, Randolph painstakingly approached the subjects of 22 references in Waugh's letters and postcards, which his lawyers considered to be defamatory, and succeeded in getting clearance for 20 of them. He certainly did not intend this to be a posthumous work. Melvin Lasky. editor of *Encounter* (in whose June issue they will appear), tells me: "He was talking to me about it only three weeks ago – he had just made the final proof corrections when he died'.

Many of Waugh's most pointed thrusts were directed against his correspondent. Having just emerged from the Brompton Hospital in 1946 after the removal of part of a lung, Randolph learnt from a third party that "Your nice friend Captain Waugh ... is fulminating against the medical profession, which he says with its customary ineptitude removed the only part of you which was not malignant." Of Winston Churchill Jr's wedding in a register office, he writes tartly: "When your son marries like a Christian, I will certainly send him a present. Registration at a government office does not demand munificence." (*1968*)

"I can't say I recognise
any of them."

FOOD AND DRINK

Slimming World magazine is looking for a food editor, reports a recruitment website. As you would expect, the job is only part-time. (2014)

. . .

The advent of the Breathalyser is introducing a new field of connoisseurship to the post-prandial scene. Witness this conversation culled from the slightly melancholy finale to a recent Surrey dinner party:

> Guest: This is a very pleasant glass of water.
> Host: Yes—it is soft and mellow and very easy on the palate.
> Guest: Who is your supplier?
> Host: It is East Surrey Water. It is best slightly chilled. What do you drink ?
> Guest: Metropolitan water. It is slightly harder and lacks the gentle character and smoothness of East Surrey.
> Host: Let me give you a couple of bottles to take home with you. Don't forget to chill it.
> (1967)

. . .

After six years as Mr Carson, the butler in *Downton Abbey*, Jim Carter has polished his last fishknife and poured his last port. For some actors, a big role like that can be all-consuming, but Carter reveals that his wife, Imelda Staunton, wishes he were so domesticated in real life. "My wife complains that I don't take my work home with me," he says. (2015)

A lunch is a high spot of the annual meeting of the Bank for International Settlements in Basle. This time they fortified themselves against depression – if not inflation – with foie gras, smoked ham, contre-filet of beef and a mountain of strawberries and ice cream, washed down with several vintage wines. After all this, our man on the spot says, the problems of sterling somehow seemed less worrying – until the market opened next morning. (1966)

· · ·

As the nation's fatties begin their latest short-lived new year's diet, some useful advice is offered in the Weight Watchers terms and conditions: "You do not have to accept cookies to use our website." No mention of whether you can get away with accepting cheese. (2015)

· · ·

Look: it's a Nick Griffin-themed bottle of BNP-endorsed "Cornish wine" for sale on the party's website[40]. What chic dinner party could do without? It comes in any colour, as long as it's white. Or, controversially, red. "Actually," confesses the winemaker Peter Mullins, "we import most of the grapes from Canada." (2006)

· · ·

After last week's item about the trouble that Andrew Strauss had in managing Phil Tufnell, his cricket team-mate, another story about the pair involves Tufnell for once being first to training. "What's the problem, Tuffers?" his captain asked. "Well, my wife went out for some milk and hasn't come home. I think she's left me." Strauss asked

---

[40] The British National Party, a far-right nationalist party, led from 1999 to 2014 by Griffin.

how he was coping. "Oh fine," Tufnell replied. "I've got some of that powdered stuff." (2014)

. . .

There seems no end to the fun people are getting from the Sex Discrimination Act. Anthony Blunt, chairman of the firm that makes Gentleman's Relish – a classy and spicy kind of fish paste – says an apparently serious complaint has been made about the discriminatory nature of the name. He tells me that a reader of a women's magazine asked the magazine to check with the Equal Opportunities' Commission whether the name offended against the Act. The reply was that it did not, so long as the product was sold freely to both sexes. "They said we came in the same category as Daddies' Sauce," said Blunt, a bit petulantly. "That riled us a bit. They're pretty down market." Daddies' were not too happy about Blunt's comment. "We may be down market," said a spokesman, "but we sell ten times as much as they do." Now, girls ... (1976)

. . .

Another prop of the British way of life has given way. The French are actually drinking twice as much port as we are: 40 per cent of the Portuguese exports going to them, only 20 per cent to us. One explanation is that the lower end of the British market now settles for port-type wine from South Africa, Cyprus or New Zealand. However, all is not lost: 95 per cent of exports of vintage port still come to Britain. This news comes from João Brito e Cunha, President of the Port Wine Institute of Oporto, who yesterday presented bottles of port dated 1854 and 1871 to the Lord Mayor of London, Sir Charles Trinder. He assured Sir Charles that the wine would be drinkable in about a month, when it had recovered from the journey. The golden (or ruby) years for port in this country were 1880-90 and 1925-32, when Britain took 65 per cent. Demand fell after the last war, when many of the younger people could not get port and lost, or did not acquire, the taste for it. (1969)

• • •

Proprietor Peter Boizot's unflappable response when police warned lunchers of a possible incendiary device in Kettner's champagne bar in Soho last week: "If anyone wants to leave, would you mind settling your bills first?" (1984)

• • •

Liverpool City Council, once home to Derek Hatton's Militant Tendency, has gone soft. The Liberal Democrat regime issued the following politically correct memo on plans for 24-hour drinking: "The current cultural practice of migrating from one licensed premises to another and then another..." Does it mean a "pub crawl"? (2003)

• • •

Hazy memories of foreign protocol come from the bustling MP for Edgbaston, Dame Jill Knight, in her new book *About the House*. In 1967, she was one of a delegation to Russia, and she recounts the meal at the Kremlin. Her mistake was to take a sip of vodka, then resume her seat. A stentorian monosyllable split the air: "YOU!!" bellowed a comrade. "You have insult ... Finish drink." She did, nervously, only to be refilled eight times. "To tell the truth, I do not normally have eight vodkas at lunch," she explains. By the end she was so drunk that she smashed her crystal glass. "Every man rose to his feet to toast me. After that, I cheerfully smashed my way round the Soviet Union." (1995)

The cabinet may or may not be united over the imminent round of spending cuts, but it is definitely divided by its tastes in wine. John Patten, the secretary of state for education, is letting it be known that he has nothing but contempt for the cellar he inherited from his predecessor, Kenneth Clarke. Patten's favourite after-dinner story concerns the six bottles of rioja he found languishing in the ministerial cupboard on his first day in office. "It was of such excruciating quality," he says, "that I decided the only way to get rid of it was to invite the general secretaries of the teaching unions for lunch and inflict it on them." (1992)

• • •

When Clement Freud ran a nightclub in the 1950s he believed that as the taste of wine was subjective, no one would have the courage to make a really sustained complaint. As a consequence when any customer looked askance after an initial taste of the wine he had ordered, Freud would instantly remove it mumbling apologies. "I then served him the bottle the last person had complained about," he says. (1988)

"Hold the front page! It's a leak of a press release of a briefing on the Pre-Budget Report!"

THE MEDIA

As chief whip, Michael Gove will hear some creative excuses from colleagues in awkward situations, but few will show the chutzpah that the young Gove is said to have displayed as a BBC reporter 20 years ago. They still sigh with admiration at Broadcasting House about the time when Gove, usually a model of expenses probity, was questioned over a receipt. "You say that you had lunch with Ken Clarke [then chancellor] on this day," Gove's boss told him. "That can't be true because I had lunch with Clarke that day." A senior BBC man tells me that Gove, quick as a flash and without blushing, replied: "You mean that Clarke had two lunches that day? The greedy bastard." (2015)

• • •

One of the Great American Shortages is paper. Less dramatic than petrol, fertilizer or heating oil, it has none the less caused supermarkets to cut down on paper bags. There was a long article about the shortage and its probable dire consequences in Saturday's *Washington Post*. That day the paper had 150 pages, the next day 448. (1973)

• • •

MPs have not read enough poetry, rued Andrew Marr at the *Radio Times* festival yesterday, describing the likes of Denis Healey as "deeply cultured" compared with today's crop. Marr has a new Radio 4 show on the history of British poetry, but will have to skip over Philip Larkin due to all the swearing. Asked if the BBC had a list of banned words, he said: "I have seen notes for dramas that say: 'There is one too many buggers, the f••• count is alright, but we could do with one less pr••k.'" It sounds like how they select the *Question Time* panel. (2015)

Fleet Street isn't what it was. Mike Molloy, who edited the *Daily Mirror* in the 1970s and 1980s, has just published an entertaining memoir called *The Happy Hack*. He had quite a motley crew working for him. When Molloy took over, the *Mirror* had a motoring correspondent who was banned from driving after failing a breath test, a gardening correspondent who only owned a window box, a slimming correspondent who was perpetually a stone and a half overweight and a travel editor who was banned from flying with British Airways after a bout of cabin rage. "There was also a delightful feature writer who hadn't written an article in five years," Molloy says. "Six years later we gave him a farewell dinner at the Ritz Hotel — and he still hadn't written anything." (2016)

• • •

I do not wish to appear to be getting at *The Daily Telegraph*, which is in many ways excellent value, but what are we to make of this extract from yesterday's editorial about York University? "It must be added that each of the five students has been found to have an emotional problem: one of them, for example, is a girl, and another lives in Northern Ireland." (1974)

• • •

Charlotte Green is surely the BBC's greatest giggler since Brian "Leg Over" Johnston. The Radio 4 newsreader's most famous corpse came in 2008 when she got it into her head that a clip of the oldest known recording of the human voice sounded like an angry bee stuck in a bottle and broke down in laughter while reading the obituary item that followed. However, in her new autobiography, *The News is Read*, Green says that the bee incident was nothing compared with a meltdown very early in her career, when she mistakenly read that the Pope had issued a "condomnation" of birth control. "I had just about got myself back on track," she writes, "only to be confronted with the financial cue that began, 'In the City, rubber prices rose sharply today'." It took several minutes before order was restored. (2014)

• • •

Gaping holes in copies of *The Times* in the House of Commons have been bewildering MPs for the past three months. But last week the culprit was finally uncovered: George Mudie, a junior education minister, has been discreetly cutting out the Books for Schools token for his wife, a head teacher. (1999)

• • •

If Ed Miliband's choice of *Angels*, the saccharine Robbie Williams hit, on *Desert Island Discs* seemed populist, host Kirsty Young agreed, telling the Radio Festival she thought his selections were 50 per cent political. Yet his was not the only tedious edition. In *For the Love of Radio 4*, a new book by Caroline Hodgson, she tells of when Alistair MacLean was invited on the show in the 1970s. As host Roy Plomley grilled his castaway, the interview kept coming back to moose and Mounties rather than MacLean's hit novels like *Where Eagles Dare*. Finally, Plomley twigged that this was not the eminent novelist, but a man of the same name who was European head of the Ontario Tourist Board. Embarrassed, they recorded the programme anyway, but never aired it. Maybe the BBC should have claimed they meant to invite David Miliband or, better still, just not broadcast Ed at all. (2014)

I am intrigued to learn that the BBC is resurrecting its general trainee scheme next year. The much coveted graduate traineeships, which brought many of the present top brass into the corporation, were axed because in the words of one senior BBC man "we found that we were recruiting and training six director-generals a year". Presumably with the present turnover of staff in the upper corridors of Broadcasting House and Television Centre, they feel that they may need that kind of number again. (1979)

. . .

A worldwide dearth of old-fashioned political dictators is depressing John Simpson, foreign news editor of the BBC and outspoken critic of the BBC's director-general, John Birt. "I adore them [dictators]," he tells the *Radio Times* this week. "The sad thing if they're becoming rarities. You have to visit weird parts of the world now to find them – like Television Centre and Broadcasting House." (1997)

. . .

The Perth conference is buzzing with a reported conversation in the Tory inner sanctum. Mrs Thatcher: "Jeffrey, what would you do after this job?" Jeffrey Archer: "Captain the English cricket team. What about you?" Mrs T: "Become a newspaper editor." Archer: "Which one?" Mrs T: "All of them, of course." (1986)

The plane carrying a Southern Television camera crew to Gambia made a refuelling stop in Casablanca. Anthony Howard, the crew's director, says armed guards met them in the transit lounge, searched them and perused their newspapers. These included such explosive stuff as the *Morning Star*, *Private Eye*, *Playboy* and *Daily Telegraph* and *Nova* but the guards ignored them and confiscated only copies of *The Times*, explaining: 'We do not allow that sort of subversive material into our country." (1974)

"Very nice, but I'm still not sure
they're 'you'"

THE ROYAL FAMILY

As the Prince and Princess of Wales continue their argument, as the Prince describes it, over what to call the baby, it is plain that they have plenty to argue about. George V, the last Prince of Wales to father offspring, had a total of five sons with a tally of 21 names. There was a John, an Alexander, an Edmund, a William, a Francis, a Charles, a Henry, a Christian, an Andrew, a Patrick and a David, two Edwards and Fredericks, and three Georges and Alberts. Edward VII's sons, with four names a piece, add Ernest and Victor to the canon.[41] (1982)

• • •

The Queen must be one of the most recognisable women in the world, but not to the Americans who once met her walking near Balmoral. Richard Griffin, the Queen's former protection officer, gave a talk recently about his work with the royals in which he described the encounter. The Queen had left her tiara at home and was not recognised in tweeds and a headscarf. "Do you live round here?" the Americans asked her. HM replied that she had a house nearby. "Have you ever met the Queen?" they asked. "No," she replied, then gestured at her policeman, "but he has." (2016)

• • •

Another job gone for ever. After 296 years, it has become impossible to find stand-ins prepared to spend 20 minutes a day winding the Curfew Tower clock at Windsor Castle for 50p a time while the regular winder is away. The clock has just been sent to Derby to be electrified at a cost of about £5,250 – or some 30 years wages. (1985)

---

[41] This was the first appearance in the Diary of Prince William, now the Duke of Cambridge.

After writing *The Queen* and *The Audience*, Peter Morgan's next take on HM's life is for the forthcoming Netflix series *The Crown*. Matt Smith, the former star of *Doctor Who*, plays the Duke of Edinburgh in it and has been given some advice by Donald Douglas, who played the duke in the 1993 TV film *Diana: Her True Story*. "I watched lots of newsreels to get the voice right," Douglas says, "but, when we came to do it, all the director kept saying was, 'Be more grumpy'." (2016)

· · ·

At a Buckingham Palace reception the Duke of Edinburgh demonstrates yet again his legendary tact. He was approached by a young woman who asked if he could design a range of tea towels for the Royal Household. The Duke fixed him with an icy stare and declared: "I don't have anything to do with the washing-up." (2005)

· · ·

Fay Weldon told an *Oldie* lunch of visiting Buckingham Palace with Beryl Bainbridge. "She couldn't smoke," recalled Weldon. "Beryl likes to. She was telling this woman what a terribly boring party it was. Someone dragged her away. You can't speak to the Queen like that!"

"Oh dear," said Bainbridge. "I thought it was Vera Lynn." (2008)

· · ·

True to her extravagant form, the Duchess of York travelled first class to New York yesterday – and she paid every penny for the luxury. "She's the only one of the royals who is always honest enough to ask for a first-class ticket," said an airline source. "The others simply buy cheap tickets and expect to be upgraded." (1996)

Well, has he got his daddy's ears? The first charming pictures of Prince William of Wales leave me in doubt. A blanket here, possibly a little help from mummy's little finger there, and an ear depressed against her dress in another. We will just have to wait and see. (1982)

• • •

I hear that even the Royal Family is feeling the economic chill. Pheasants shot on the Sandringham estate by Prince Philip, Prince Charles and Prince Edward in the past week are fetching only £2 per bird in the shops, which makes them 50p cheaper than last season's bag. Royally killed pheasant is just one more example of a British export industry which has collapsed. The Italians and Hungarians have flooded Europe with game, destroying our once-lucrative market in France. Still, their birds don't have the same class, do they? (1981)

• • •

The Queen, I hear, will be asked to pay an extra £284 in rates for Balmoral Castle next year, an increase of 8.7 per cent. She has fared better than her subjects in the area, whose rates have been upped by an average of 18 per cent. The reason, I'm told, is that Balmoral is out in the sticks and therefore deemed "less easy to rent" than property closer to oil-rich Aberdeen. (1985)

• • •

Poor Prince Charles. His parents popped into a refuge for the homeless before lunch on Britannia yesterday. As Prince Philip signed the visitors' book, he asked the Queen: "What's the date? Is it the 13th?"

"No", her Majesty replied with a granite expression. "It's the 14th. Charles's birthday." (1997)

On the morning we reported that the Duke of Edinburgh had adopted a new "limp" handshake because of the agony of shaking millions of hands, he began a visit to Cambridge University by breakfasting with its top sportsmen. Expecting something flabby and wimpish, the men got royal bone-crushers. "I almost turned blue with agony", said Olympic oarsman John Pritchard. (1985)

. . .

Ann Morrow, whose book *The Queen* is published today, says that she wants to show the warm and humorous side of the monarch's personality. She cites two examples. At one of her Buckingham Palace luncheons the Queen's guests included the actor Tom Courtenay, shortly after his performance as the Bolshevik commander in *Dr Zhivago*. Noting his shy and diffident manner, the Queen said: "Look at him. You wouldn't think he wants to overthrow society, would you?" And touring an artificial insemination unit with Sir Richard Trehane, then chairman of the Milk Marketing Board, the Queen spied a curious object in a jar. "What is that?" she asked. "That, ma'am, is a cow's vagina", Sir Richard replied. "Oh well," said the Queen lightly, "ask a silly question!" (1983)

. . .

The Prince of Wales is normally a model of restraint on official engagements. But yesterday, after sampling some of the local brew on a Devon farm, he declared: "Where are all the young farmers? I have found a new sport, pudding hurling." He then launched an orange and Cointreau pudding into the air. (2003)

Queen Elizabeth the Queen Mother is today expected to perform her first official engagement since her hip replacement before Christmas. She is due to unveil a memorial at Westminster Abbey to the Special Operations Executive which was formed as a secret service in July 1940. Although Clarence House refused yesterday to confirm her attendance, former members of the operations executive are brushing down their togs to greet her at the Abbey.

Veterans are delighted. Leo Marks, who as a stripling of 20 ran the codes for the resistance movement, spoke of her great interest in the executive. "She and the late King came to inspect our cipher artefacts once," he says. "His Majesty stood at one end of the room and we sent him a shortwave radio message, encrypted by Her Majesty. Nobody could decode it for a very long time because she had made a mistake. It became known as the Queen's mistake."

Marks told her years later that her very mistake had actually helped to crack an indecipherable code in one of the most important operations of the war.

"In the operation to blow up the Germans' heavy water plant, we couldn't decode the first message they sent us," he said. "In desperation I said, 'try the Queen's mistake.' And we cracked it – the agent had made the same mistake as Her Majesty." When she heard of her contribution to the war effort, she was modesty itself: "I'm so glad to have been of some use," she said. (1996)

"She's really taken to the idea of
performance-related pay."

ON STAGE

Lyndsey Turner's decision to begin her version of *Hamlet* at the Barbican with the prince's famous soliloquy from Act III, rather than the ghost prancing about on the rooftops, is rather odd. Was she worried that the audience might need warming up with a famous number first, like Neil Diamond opening a gig with *Sweet Caroline*? Should Benedict Chamberpot dry up one night and forget how it starts, he need only look at the front of the stalls. It is an anomaly of the Barbican theatre that the second row of seats is numbered from five to 33. There is no 2B. (2015)

• • •

Lord Birkett, who is producing the film of *A Midsummer Night's Dream*, with members of the Royal Shakespeare Company directed by Peter Hall, has arranged for 200 cabbage white butterflies to be supplied by a butterfly farm in Kent. If all goes well, they will flutter around Titania – played by Judi Dench – in the bower scene. Meanwhile, in chrysalis form they will be popped into a refrigerator, where apparently they will survive until thawed out. They will cost £17 10s – or 1s 9d each. (1967)

• • •

Stephen Sondheim, who is 86 next week, has a soft spot for audiences over here. In conversation with Rufus Norris, director of the National Theatre, the American composer said: "British audiences are different: they listen." He puts this down to Britain having "many centuries of being interested in language", unlike people in the US. Sondheim's love of language — he delights in pointing out that his surname is an anagram of "hedonism" and his full name of "he pens demon hits" — means that he gets stroppy with people who mishear his lyrics. After one critic heard "the best y'all agree" in *Follies* (1971) as "bestial", he swore to be cautious with "aural ambiguities". That didn't stop some from hearing the line "Don't you love farce?" in his *Send In the Clowns*, from *A Little Night Music* (1973), as "Don't you love farts?" (2016)

• • •

"It's remarkably unrehearsed. The lighting is appalling and the directing is even worse." Not the reviews of another doomed West End musical, but Glenda Jackson, the Labour MP for Hampstead and Highgate, and once one of Britain's most distinguished actresses, on Parliament. (2005)

• • •

Don't mess with Dame Judi Dench. All those years as M have taught her how to kill a man with her bare hands, or at least to disarm him with her tongue. In an updated version of his book *Bond on Bond*, Sir Roger Moore tells a story about the actress arguing with a taxi driver. Dench was crossing Shaftesbury Avenue on her way to a rehearsal, head full of lines, and wasn't paying much attention to traffic. A cabbie, who had to swerve to avoid her, leant out of his window and shouted: "Mind where you're going, you stupid [expletive]." Without flinching, Dench replied: "It's Dame [expletive] to you." (2015)

• • •

The racing world at Lambourn has seen some unusual sights over the years. Yet few can have matched that of Oliver Reed, the hell-raising actor, arriving drunk and naked at Newbury, on the doorstep of his ex-lover and her new husband, Gay Kindersley. According to a new biography of Kindersley, *Flings Over Fences*, by Robin Rhoderick-Jones, Reed had not forgiven the Queen Mother's amateur-jockey-turned-trainer friend for marrying Philippa Harper when he himself was smitten by her. "As it's your birthday, I've come in my birthday suit," he yelled from outside the couple's front door. (1994)

. . .

Nathan Lane, filming the Hollywood remake of *The Producers* with Uma Thurman and Matthew Broderick, had better hope that his co-stars are fonder of him than the thesps in London were. According to *The Stage*, Lane's West End colleagues were so incensed by the payment he demanded – apparently more than £50,000 a week – that a cast whip-round produced just £6 to buy a leaving present. (2005)

. . .

In an essay for *The Cricketer* on Peter O'Toole's love of the sport, Michael Henderson spins a tale of Richard Burton, O'Toole's drinking buddy, who was found by a group of actors loafing in front of the Tavern bar at Lord's. The day passed, drink followed drink, until one actor asked whether Burton should be tootling off to the Old Vic, where he was due to perform that night. Burton scoffed: "It's only Iago."

While only Hamlet and Richard III have more lines in Shakespeare, he had a point. This was a production of *Othello* in which he and John Neville were alternating the lead roles. If it had been his night to play *Othello*, he would have needed longer in make-up. (2014)

. . .

Translating Shakespeare for foreign audiences — even those who speak English — can be tricky, says Greg Doran, artistic director of the Royal Shakespeare Company. He told *The Stage* that he was directing *A Midsummer Night's Dream* in upstate New York when a young man came up to him with a classic edition of the play and said he thought the Bard's first name was William. "I said it was," Doran recalled, "and he said, 'But it says on the cover that it's Pelican Shakespeare'." (2015)

· · ·

The *Daily Mail*'s repeated assertions that the Russian theatre director Yuri Lyubimov was under armed guard in London after his bitter attack on Soviet authorities in an interview with *The Times* exaggerated the drama. On Tuesday it was our deputy arts editor, Bryan Appleyard, who was mistaken by the company at the Lyric Theatre, Hammersmith, for a secret service minder of the heavy sort. Appleyard spent seven hours with Lyubimov and his family that day, and saw no armed guard protecting them. He did, though, spot the KGB man covering the Soviet embassy official on his rendezvous with Lyubimov. When Lyubimov's Hungarian wife was sent to see whether the Russians had arrived for the meeting in the theatre bar Appleyard asked how she would recognize them. "She can smell them," Lyubimov's interpreter replied succinctly (1983)

· · ·

London theatre audiences are notoriously hard to please. "On Broadway, the star gets an automatic standing ovation; in the West End they don't," Kathleen Turner tells *Time Out*, although that may have something to do with the legroom in our Victorian theatres and the fear that if everyone stands at once it may literally bring the house down. Turner goes on to tell a story about when Dustin Hoffman played Shylock in *The Merchant of Venice* over here and was asked to announce at the curtain call that Laurence Olivier had just passed away. For once, the audience rose straight to their feet. Turner claims

181

that as Hoffman walked off, he muttered: "You have to die; you have to f•••ing die ..." (2014)

• • •

Robert Morley presided ebulliently over a cast list of theatrical stars yesterday at a Foyle's lunch for the publication of *Change Lobsters and Dance*, by the German-born actress Lilli Palmer. "Most of them are working," said Morlev as he called the roll for the benefit of the audience. "I'm not, which is why I am here." Miss Palmer's book, he said, had already sold 500,000 hardback copies in Germany. "It shows old Germany isn't finished, despite what they all say. He recounted a story of meeting "one of Miss Palmer's changed lobsters", her former husband, Rex Harrison. "I had just appeared on *This Is Your Life* and Rex Harrison said God forbid that it should ever happen to him. But then he said I had the right sort of life. 'One house, one wife, and if you will forgive me saying so, Robert, one performance'." (1976)

• • •

When Timothy West appears with his wife, Prunella Scales, at the Mermaid Theatre on Tuesday, to give a lunchtime show of extracts from Shakespeare, he will no doubt be hoping to avoid the sort of contretemps that blighted an earlier Shakespearian excursion. He was in Egypt last year, on a tour with productions of *Hamlet* and *Antony and Cleopatra*, and a performance of the latter was planned on a stage in front of the Sphinx. Delighted by the setting, the players were even more pleased when they were told that the pyramids could be illuminated during Alexandrian scenes in the play.

However, an emissary from the British Embassy explained that another production of *Antony and Cleopatra* was being performed in Cairo, an amateur show featuring members of the embassy staff. He asked if it was possible for the professionals not to provide competition. So, diplomatically, the actors took to the stage in front of the Sphinx and performed ... *Hamlet*, complete with illuminated pyramids. (1978)

• • •

Catherine Zeta-Jones and Michael Douglas may be Hollywood's golden couple. But their two-year-old son, Dylan, is a Hollywood child to the core. Not only can he belt out the chorus of *All That Jazz* but the toddler magically stops crying if Zeta-Jones yells: "And the Oscar goes to ... Dylan Douglas." Zeta-Jones revealed in an interview with *People* magazine that her son has a talent for mimicry: "He does a Prince Charles walk." (2003)

• • •

King Lear is often cited as the theatre's toughest role, but the real challenge comes after the old man has coughed his last. "Once you've played Lear, nobody offers you anything else," says Timothy West, who won rave reviews for the role at the Old Vic this year. "Anthony Hopkins had to go to Hollywood and Robert Stephens died." But West, 68, wants to do something modern and edgy and modern. "The problem is that nearly every new play is about the individual. I want to do something that deals with the way events impact on communities." Is *EastEnders* out of the question?[42] (2003)

---

[42] In fact, West joined the cast of EastEnders, the BBC soap opera, ten years later.

Irving Wardle[43] coupled the names of Shakespeare and Chekhov in *The Times* on Wednesday as Britain's favourite dramatists, They were also linked by Tolstoy, though less flatteringly; I heard the story from Camille Honig, editor of *Mediterranean Review*, who was told it by his friend Leonid Pasternak (father of Boris), who in turn got it from Chekhov himself. Out walking with the playwright one day, Tolstoy turned on him with good-humoured anger: "Anton Pavlovitch, what is the matter with you? You are an intelligent man, a talented man and a good man. How is it that you write such bad, such trivial plays? Aren't you ashamed to write such silly plays?"

Chekhov recalled: "I felt so embarrassed and miserable that I was utterly speechless. I didn't know which way to turn. But I felt considerably relieved when at the end of our walk, Tolstoy stopped and, after a dramatic silence, added: 'Why, my dear Anton Pavlovitch, your plays are so stupid, so meaningless ... why, they are ... they are even worse than Shakespeare!'" (1970)

• • •

The late, great Tommy Cooper bought the house down at the *Oldie* literary lunch at Simpsons in the Strand yesterday. The comedian Barry Cryer recalled his quick-thinking when on National Service he fell asleep on sentry duty. "Cautiously opening one eye, Tommy realised that the regimental sergeant-major was standing in front of him, so he clamped it shut again immediately and said, very seriously, 'Amen'." (2003)

---

[43]   Drama critic of *The Times*, 1963-89.

Terry Waite's fellow beardo Brian Blessed has just started frightening children in the new musical version of *Chitty Chitty Bang Bang*, but he seems to be a little insecure about his role. "I leave in three weeks," he told me of his role as Baron Bomburst. "They think I'm hopeless, can't wait to get rid of me. And why wouldn't they with this voice? I was terrible. You think so, don't you? No, tell me."

I've been an admirer of Brian since Flash Gordon, so thought it best to play along. I agree, you were terrible, you really stank. "You, sir, have ruined my night," Blessed suddenly exploded in genuine rage. "This was the greatest first night of my life. I've never had such an audience reaction and it has been utterly destroyed. You've depressed me, told me I'm hopeless. Good night." (2002)

• • •

A top gag from Sir Tim Rice. Celebrity Jack asked him for details regarding the fabled split with Lord Lloyd-Webber. To which Sir Tim replied: "Would you want to work with a guy who wanted 75 per cent of the credit? Would you want to work with a guy who wanted 75 per cent of the money? Would you want to work with a guy who tried to bonk every leading lady in every show? Well, neither did Andrew." (2000)

• • •

A London theatre is holding open auditions for a role in its Christmas production of *The Pied Piper*. Hopefuls should be light on their feet, possess a lean and cunning look and bring their own tail. The Unicorn Arts Theatre is appealing for a rat from the public because it says it can't afford to rent a professional plus its handler at the going rate of £150 an hour. "We want the Olivier of the rodent world. Candidates should be easy to handle, good-looking and well-mannered," says the theatre. "But we do not discriminate between colour, gender or age: we would like to hear from any rat." (1995)

· · ·

Productions of the Open Air Theatre at Regent's Park are accustomed to competing with the roar of lions from nearby London Zoo. But a performance of the current *Macbeth*, which was competing with a party at a zoo, had to be temporarily suspended, when the main fight scene was interrupted by the wafting tones of John Lennon's *Give Peace a Chance*. (1991)

· · ·

Observing the strictest constitutional properties, Mrs Thatcher was still prime minister at the Shaftesbury Theatre throughout Tuesday night. Only during yesterday's matinee performance, after John Major had visited the Palace, did Ray Cooney, author and director of the political farce *Out of Order*, change all "Maggie" references in the script to "Young Johnny". (1990)

· · ·

Roy Dotrice is insuring against gas cuts by carrying his own supply around with him in a large canister. He needs it to light the coal fire he has on stage in his one-man show, *Brief Lives*. In it Dotrice portrays John Aubrey, reminiscing and rambling in front of the flickering flames. Today the chief of the Richmond-on-Thames fire service is going to inspect the safety of Dotrice's incendiary arrangements before allowing him to open in the Theatre on the Green tonight. Dotrice is so pleased with his gas-can that he is taking it with him on his next foreign tour, to Colorado. Fire has also been giving Jimmy Edwards theatrical problems. While he was off-stage in Newcastle, where he is appearing in *Big Bad Mouse* with Eric Sykes, he looked across the road and saw that his hotel, "The Royal Turk's Head", was burning. He ran on stage, and bellowed through his moustache: "The hotel is on fire." The audience just laughed, while his luggage went on burning. (1973)

RELIGION

Canon Andrew White returned to his parish in Baghdad this week. Vicar of the only Anglican church in Iraq, he has lost 1,000 parishioners in the past year, murdered by Islamic militants, but will stay to help those in need. White once applied for a parish in London but was told that because he suffers from multiple sclerosis an urban posting would probably be "too stressful" for him. (2014)

• • •

David Bowie died this week "surrounded by his family", a phrase that appears so often in the obituaries of famous people that you sometimes wonder whether they shuffled off in order to get a bit of peace. James Runcie, the novelist, tells me that when his father, the former archbishop of Canterbury, passed away in 2000 he was also described as being "surrounded by his family", even though it was untrue.

Runcie, whose *Grantchester* novels (starring James Norton) will get a second series on ITV this spring, says that he was reading psalms to his father on his deathbed. "After about ten of them, I got bored and went to pour myself a large whisky," he said. "He died while I was out of the room drinking it. I think he was waiting for me to go away." (2016)

• • •

It's been a few days since I ran an episcopal story. John Griffith sent one about two businessmen on a train, sitting opposite a bishop, all doing the Times2 crossword. One businessman says to the other: "I'm stuck on 17 across. Clue: 'female'. Four letters, ends U, N, T." His companion answers: "That's easy: aunt." At this, the bishop puts down his pencil, leans across and says: 'Excuse me, could I borrow a rubber?'" (2015)

That the Archbishop of Canterbury chose not to wear his Military Cross at the Falklands service in St Paul's should not be regarded as being of special significance in the row over the supposed "wetness" of his sermon. Runcie, who won the medal by rescuing a man from a blazing tank in the front line while serving under Willie Whitelaw in the Scots Guards, has never worn his medals with his ecclesiastical dress: "He prefers not to," I was told by Lambeth Palace yesterday. And yes, the Archbishop did write the sermon himself, which I add because, when it finished, Edward Heath turned to Michael Foot and asked if he had provided the script. (1982)

• • •

The Easter message went astray at a church in York when a printer made four banners for them proclaiming "Chris is Risen". A case of "More T, vicar?" The church curate suggested that the printers may have been confusing them with the nearby baptist church. "Their pastor is called Chris and he has to be up for a 6.30am service on Sunday," Ned Lunn said. "His predecessor didn't manage to get up for the service last year." (2016)

• • •

With the Boat Race on tomorrow, the Archbishop of Canterbury may think wistfully back 40 years to when he was briefly in the Cambridge crew. A month before the 1975 race, Cambridge's cox fell ill and their bow, Chris Langridge, was asked to find a replacement. Going into lunch at Trinity, he spotted a young Justin Welby, who at that stage of his life was taking Psalm 23's line about being led beside still waters a bit too literally, and asked if he would step in.

For three days, Welby steered the boat and Langridge is convinced that if the future archbishop had trialled the next year he would have got in. Another oarsman recalls: "He had nerves of steel, which he used to lure a chasing boat into the bank by deliberately cornering at the last possible moment." All good preparation for the Church, perhaps. I'm told these days Welby likes to compare coxes to Thomas Hobbes' description of the life of man: "Nasty, brutish and short."

An archbishop hasn't yet competed in the Boat Race but a future bishop rowed for Oxford in the 1930s. In 1951, Gerald Ellison, by then bishop of Willesden, umpired the race, but he must have upset the Almighty since Oxford sank soon after the start. (2015)

• • •

The lords spiritual have been dabbling in politics recently, with interventions on refugees and tax credits that may get them bumped off the Downing Street Christmas card list. An alternative view of the noble bishops is reported in *Who Goes Home?*, a parliamentary miscellany by Robert Rogers, the former clerk of the Commons. He recalls an advertising poster that claimed "80 per cent of bishops take *The Times*". Underneath, someone had scribbled: "The other 20 per cent buy it." (2015)

• • •

I wrote yesterday about St Paul's cathedral's envy that Canterbury has more relics. It led Graham Cory to write in with the story of a visitor to a cathedral in northern Italy who was told that they owned the skull of St Peter. That's odd, the visitor said. A cathedral in the south of the country also claims to own St Peter's skull. "Ah," the guide replied. "But this is his skull when he was a young man." (2015)

Steve Williams sends a tale about the Bishop of Lichfield investigating the scale of prostitution in Walsall. He was accompanied on a tour round the town by a young curate and on seeing their first street-walker the bishop exclaimed: "What an eyesore." The curate was not sure how to react to this, so kept quiet until they turned a street and saw two more. "Look Your Grace," he piped up. "A pair of nice whores." (2015)

• • •

The Revd Richard Coles, the media tart vicar, spoke with affection of when he used to live in London's King's Cross, in its more seamy days, "with its street corners filled with women waiting for a bus that never seemed to come". The area has since been gentrified. "The last time I visited it was noticeably tarted up," Coles said. "Or rather, tarted down." (2014)

• • •

Not wishing to offend the Archbishop of Canterbury during his present tour, Australian officials wired Terry Waite, his assistant, to ask how much of their shapely Sheilas should be exposed to archiepiscopal view. They pointed out that one city on his schedule had a north and south beach, which would Dr Runcie prefer "bearing in mind that the north has topless sunbathing"? Waite cabled back: "Don't worry, the archbishop always sunbathes topless." (1985)

The Bishop of Leeds, Nick Baines, published a few World Cup prayers on his blog on Saturday. The first three are for a good tournament, for Brazil and for people who have no interest in the blessed thing — "grant us the gift of sympathy" — but the fourth, for the England team itself, seems pretty apt. It consists of only two words: "Oh God ..." (2014)

• • •

Jeremy Paxman has harangued most of the leading political figures of the past 30 years, but the one he chose to recall at the Political Cartoon of the Year awards this week was an odd encounter with the Dalai Lama, which began with the Lama expounding on the evils of bacon and masturbation while they were waiting to record. Sounds like a ham-fisted way of breaking the ice.

A short while after the interview, His Holiness came back to the room. "I've lost my treasures," he complained. Paxo dutifully had a look around and found a purple bag under the table. The Lama was so happy that he insisted "you must have one of my treasures" and, as Paxman began to demur, pressed something into his hand. "It turned out," Paxo said, "that this living god's treasure was a Werther's Original." (2014)

• • •

Wanted: a new aide for George Carey, the Archbishop of Canterbury. Must have sound judgment and enthusiastic commitment. Belief in God not required. Thus reads a job description from the Church of England. "There is no need for applicants to be baptised," says a large cassock in the archbishop's office. Mind you, as the position is for a spin-doctor, a godless atheist would be perfect. (1998)

It's World Book Night today, the grown-up version of World Book Day, in which children go to school dressed as their favourite literary characters. A few weeks ago we attended a Palm Sunday procession in which the priest was wearing a long red cope. My five-year-old daughter looked puzzled at him. "Is it World Book Day again?" she asked. "Is that why Father William has come dressed as Superman?" (2016)

"I went to the chamber last week
— it's a lot smaller than it looks
on TV."

COMMONS
PEOPLE

A longboat full of Vikings, promoting the new British Museum exhibition, was seen sailing past the Palace of Westminster yesterday. Famously uncivilised, destructive and rapacious, with an almost insatiable appetite for rough sex and heavy drinking, the MPs nonetheless looked up for a bit to admire the vessel. (2014)

• • •

Always good to hear a Wodehouse quote deployed in parliament. Addressing the plodding Chris Grayling, leader of the Commons, Chris Bryant, his shadow, quoted from PGW's *The Small Bachelor*: "If men were dominoes, he would be the double-blank." (2016)

• • •

Six members of the House of Commons expenditure committee and three officials flew to Washington at the weekend, first class by Pan American, to spend a week looking at how the Americans economise on public expenditure. It would no doubt be a cheap and unworthy jibe to suggest that one way might be to cut down on the number of expensive foreign trips. (1977)

• • •

There are more men called Andrew, David and John in senior positions at FTSE 100 companies than there are women, said Peter Kyle, MP for Hove, in the Commons. "What are you going to do about it?" he asked the women's minister, Caroline Dinenage. As she rose, one backbencher shouted: "Change the names of the men." (2016)

When the Criminal Justice Bill finished its committee stage yesterday, Tory committee member Greg Knight added to the exchange of thanks to members by making a small presentation. To the consternation of all present, Knight, home office minister David Mellor's PPS, stood up and thanked Labour's home affairs spokesman, Clive Soley, for keeping MPs awake – not by the brilliance of his oratory but the garishness of his outfits. Knight thereupon whipped out a hideous tangerine shirt with black stripes and presented it to Soley as a token of his appreciation. Soley could do nothing but politely accept it. (1987)

. . .

We almost had a by-election in Chesham & Amersham yesterday after *The Sun*'s political editor accidentally dropped his mobile phone from the press balcony. It narrowly missed the head of Cheryl Gillan, who was standing next to Margaret Beckett. She kindly returned it to a mortified Tom Newton-Dunn with the words: "A little to the left and you would have killed two birds with one phone." (2016)

. . .

Tory MP Peter Thurnham swears he will tell nothing but the truth when he is quizzed by the Commons select committee on employment next week. He has agreed to be wired up to a polygraph as part of the committee's examination of the use of lie detectors to vet GCHQ staff. He tells me he expects to face "the sort of questions to make you twitch", including "Have you ever fiddled your expenses?" and "Have you ever told a lie?" Curiously, no one else on the committee has volunteered. (1984)

Fly-tieing classes are in progress at the House of Commons in preparation for the annual charity fishing match in Sussex when MPs challenge a team from the Salmon and Trout Association. The MPs will be led, as usual, by Sir Geoffrey Johnson Smith. His colleagues' fondest memory of last year's match is that Johnson Smith was persuaded to attach a delicate light leader to his line. He then promptly hooked an overweight trout, which had him running up and down the bank as he tried to land it, crying: "I have no faith in my leader." (1983)

• • •

The government whips have made an amusing addition to the decorations in their L-shaped room at 12 Downing Street: a white-faced stuffed owl in a glass case. The choice of owl is explained by the question David Mitchell, MP for Basingstoke, as a newcomer to the whips' team asked Britain Batsford, a deputy chief whip at that time when the Conservatives were in opposition: "What on earth is one expected to do as an assistant whip except sit on the front bench all day long looking like a stuffed owl?"

The spectacled Mitchell was thereafter nicknamed "the Owl", and the question would sometimes be asked: "Who's to be the stuffed owl (duty whip) tonight?" After the election Batsford sought out a suitably wide-eyed owl as a memento of the days in opposition. He calls the bird: Opposition Whip 1964-67. (1970)

A number of Tory MPs in Brighton this week are on the select committee charged with setting up the experimental televising of the Commons. They have recently returned from a fact-finding trip to Canada, whose parliament has now been televised for ten years. They recount how the Speaker of the Canadian parliament welcomed them as they watched prime minister's questions from the public gallery and announced the reason for their visit. There was an immediate hue and cry. Canadian MPs of every political hue turned as one to the gallery and yelled: "Don't do it!" For the record, no Canadian administration has been re-elected since the cameras were introduced. (1988)

• • •

Imagine the prickly unease when news of the Heseltine resignation[44] reached the pink ears of the parliamentary skiing team, ensconced halfway up a Swiss mountain near the resort of Davos. Rumours and gossip that the government was about to fall were rife. The next day the parliamentarians, including Winston Churchill and Sir John Osborne, were having lunch when a phone call was announced for another of the party, Michael Alison, Mrs T's parliamentary secretary. Alison returned ashen-faced from the telephone. "Oh, my God!" he gasped. "I have been demoted a ski school class." (1986)

• • •

Saddest entry in the Commons' register of members' interests? Labour MP Joe Ashton lists his declarable shareholdings as "Two shares in Sheffield Wednesday football club (no dividend paid since 1935)." (1987)

---

[44] Michael Heseltine, then defence secretary, resigned after an argument with the prime minister over the future of Westland Helicopters.

"Right, everyone — we're
going to have a game of
musical thrones."

MUSIC

Glam rock wasn't always especially glamorous. In a talk to college students in Boston in 1999, David Bowie recalled his early days as Ziggy Stardust, playing in a string of grotty clubs where you had "a rock act, then a stripper — sometimes one and the same".

One night he was desperate to use the loo and tottered on his platform heels backstage to ask for directions. The promoter sent him off down a corridor to where there was a sink on the wall. "There you go, use that," he said. "My good man," Bowie replied, "I am not taking a p••• in the sink." This grandeur did not go down well. "Listen son," the promoter snarled. "If it's good enough for Shirley Bassey, it's good enough for you." (2016)

• • •

The new Beatles LP, *Sergeant Pepper's Lonely Hearts Club Band*, offers a nice surprise to anybody who forgets to lift the needle at the end. When the last track, *A Day in the Life*, finishes there is a short pause and suddenly, on the run-out grooves, the Beatles are heard singing again, a six-note phrase which repeats itself automatically, as long as the needle stays in the groove, to words which sound like "I never could see any of them". This must be the first time that a record has deliberately put this final groove to musical effect. George Martin, the Beatles' recording manager, tells me that the EMI engineers thought he had taken leave of his senses when he explained what he wanted, but fans are delighting in this novelty.

It is not the only one. During one of the recording sessions Paul McCartney suggested that they should include a track especially for dogs. And so, in the pause after *Day in the Life*, there is an electronic note pitched at 13 kilocycles, a whistle inaudible to the human ear, and outside the range of modest record-players, but on high fidelity equipment a loud and clear call to all dogs. (1967)

The etiquette of dealing with anti-social fellow travellers has always been tricky. Alan Civil, the late doyen of British horn players, had his own stylish method. Travelling on the London underground during his time as principal horn with the BBC Symphony Orchestra, Civil found himself next to a blaring personal stereo. Tapping his neighbour on the shoulder, the musician asked whether the gentleman would mind turning down the volume. "It's a free world, isn't it?" came the reply, to which Civil nodded his head, reached for his instrument and proceeded to give the entire carriage a rendition of the rondo from Mozart's Horn Concerto No 4. (1992)

• • •

An exhibition of Rolling Stones memorabilia opened this week at London's Saatchi Gallery but almost all the women associated with the band were absent. No Marianne Faithfull, Anita Pallenberg et al. One woman, though, has remained a constant. Shirley Watts has been married to Charlie, the drummer, for 52 years. His passion, she says, is not music but cricket. One day he appeared in his living room in the full MCC fig — striped jacket and tie, white flannels, white shoes and cap. "Why are you dressed up for the cricket? It's not until tomorrow," Shirley asked. "I know," he replied. "But I'm practising." (2016)

• • •

John Major, the hapless social security minister whose controversial heating allowances for the old briefly made him public enemy No 1 during the cold snap, has a special interest in seeing the Royal Opera House pull free from its financial doldrums: his opera-buff wife Norma publishes a biography of Joan Sutherland in May.

During her research, Major's love of opera has come on apace. It is just as well. On their first date in 1970, Major, then a Lambeth councillor, took Norma to Covent Garden for a gala concert. The evening's peak was reached when Miss Sutherland took the stage to perform the mad scene from *Lucia di Lammermoor*. As the notes soared, Norma turned to share her rapture. To her horror she discovered her future-beloved – exhausted by a succession of late-night meetings – slumped in profound sleep.[45] (1987)

• • •

George Harrison and Spike Milligan enjoyed an odd friendship. The Beatle, who funded and made an oft-overlooked cameo with Milligan in Monty Python's *The Life of Brian*, was a fan of *The Goon Show* and once gave Spike a Fender guitar. But by the early 1980s Milligan grew frustrated at George's failure to return his phone calls. At a Letters of Note live event, the actor Andrew Scott read a letter from Milligan to Harrison dated 1983, in which the pouting ex-Goon wrote: "The funeral takes place at Golders Green Crematorium. No flowers please, just money. You will recognise me, I am the dead one." (2015)

• • •

You can't keep a world-renowned pianist down. Alfred Brendel emerged from his self-imposed retirement for one night only to appear at a gala concert in aid of Classic Relief. He sat at the piano, performed precisely one chord – A minor – and departed, to great applause. The knowledgeable Southbank audience had, of course, immediately recognised the opening to Grieg's Piano Concerto. (2009)

---

[45] This was the first appearance in the Diary of Sir John Major.

Carol Decker, the lead singer of T'Pau, who are about to release their first new album for 15 years, was reminiscing to TMS about the band's glory years. "We did the Prince's Trust a few times and I was next to Princess Diana in a photocall when the photographer said: 'Everybody say cheese.'" At this, Diana muttered "bitch" in Decker's ear. She was being helpful, though, not rude. "Say bitch," Diana clarified. "You get a sexier smile." (2014)

. . .

Preparations for Fleetwood Mac's latest comeback tour have been derailed by an industrial tambourine injury. "I strained my right arm doing arm curls, which I never do," says Stevie Nicks, 60. I'm trying to get it back so I can comfortably and enjoyably play tambourine." Life with the soft rockers is "like joining the National Guard and being deployed to Iraq in two weeks", the singer claims. (2009)

. . .

Bono has revealed that he once had to separate Bob Geldof from Tony Blair, after the ragged-trousered philanthropist grew so irate that Bono feared he was going to start spitting. "I have seen Geldof try to bite prime ministers," says the U2 frontman. It must have been John Major. Thatcher, surely, would have bitten back. (2006)

. . .

After 19 years of melodic, and relentlessly middle-of-the-road pop, the Beautiful South have split up. In a statement released yesterday the Hull-based band blamed "musical similarities" for their decision to call it a day. Full marks for originality. For that, at least. (2007)

The key to George V's admiration for Sir Edward Elgar was revealed yesterday by actor Sir Ralph Richardson when presenting prizes to music students at Wigmore Hall. "Elgar was the sort of person who looked like a bookie," he said. "In fact, that was the secret of his success with King George V. They used to go to concerts together, sit in the back row and talk about racing." (1967)

• • •

Launching the Queen's Golden Jubilee Concert at Buckingham Palace in June, Nicholas Kenyon was pleased to be correctly billed yesterday as director of the BBC Proms. "The last time I did a TV interview the caption didn't give my full title," he told journalists. "It said: 'A bald man speaks'." (2002)

• • •

Denied entry to Cave du Roi nightclub in St Tropez recently was the British singer, George Michael. On introducing himself to the bouncer, Michael was told: "I remember you from the 1980s. You're just going to have to wait until you're a name again." The bouncer looked very pleased with his joke. (1997)

• • •

Ground control to John Major: the former PM's father inspired David Bowie to write *Space Oddity*, his seminal sixties anthem. Bowie tells me that he wrote about "Major Tom," the doomed astronaut, after remembering a fading theatre bill advertising Tom Major's circus act. When Bowie wrote the tune in 1969, Tom Major-Ball was living in Brixton, having left the circus to run his faltering gnome enterprise, and the singer – yet to grace the hit parade – was strumming in nearby Bermondsey. (1999)

In the course of its 13,000-mile tour of the United States, the Royal Philharmonic Orchestra has been making a social experiment: presenting special batons to city mayors and dignitaries. In the course of one of these ceremonies a city official was having great difficulty in pronouncing the name of one of the RPO conductors, Vaclav Neumann. He was about to give up the struggle when Elgar Howarth, the orchestra's chairman, suggested: "Simply say Norman with a Bronx accent." (1968)

• • •

Sergiu Comissiona conducted the New Philharmonic in the prelude from Wagner's *Tristan and Isolde* at the Festival Hall last night. It was such a programme that got him in trouble with the local sheriff in Denver, Colorado, recently. Comissiona was on the telephone to Gothenburg, where he is musical director, and agreed a programme including the prelude. After replacing the receiver, he decided the programme was too short and so hurried round to the Western Union office to dispatch the following cable: "I want also Isolde's Death." The girl at the counter paled and kept him talking while they fetched the sheriff for a full investigation. (1972)

PEERS

If you thought that the 5p plastic bag levy was controversial, best hope that Ed Miliband ignores a bright suggestion by one of his Labour peers to impose a penny tax on every e-mail sent. Speaking in a House of Lords debate on the first 25 years of the World Wide Web, Lord Puttnam, the film producer, noted that there were 183 billion e-mails sent in the world every day and suggested that this was an untapped resource. "Last year, the need of Unicef was £1.7 billion — this tiny 1p levy could totally change the landscape of aid," he said. And spam e-mail. Puttnam admitted it was "rather late in the day to suggest this" but said that there would be one extra advantage of such a tax. "It might allow people to pause momentarily before hitting that dreadful 'Reply to All' button." (2014)

. . .

Lord Lloyd-Webber has withdrawn his motion about music in schools in the House of Lords tomorrow, after reading in this column that it clashed with the biggest date in the parliamentary choir's history. For the first time in more than 900 years, there will be a paying concert in Westminster Hall, attended by the Prince of Wales. The composer quickly realised that anybody even remotely interested in music would be in Westminster Hall rather than listening to him droning on in the Lords. (2003)

. . .

The asking price for a parliamentary question may be £1,000[46], but gaining the interest of members of the House of Lords is a rather more affordable exercise, as the RSPCA discovered after lobbying peers about factory farming. Lord Beaumont of Whitley sounds convinced.

---

[46] A reference to the Cash for Questions affair, in which MPs were alleged to have taken bribes from a lobbying firm to table questions in the Commons.

"It's the only time I have attended a launch meeting in the Grand Committee room and come away with half a pound of bacon." (1994)

• • •

Lord Bradford launches his first book today: *My Private Parts and The Stuffed Parrot.* Dirty-mac readers should restrain themselves. It is a children's book, compiled of bread-and-butter notes sent by youngsters to Lord Bradford after visiting his stately home, Weston Park, Shropshire. The title – and indeed the book – was inspired by a young girl, who, after touring his 105-roomed mansion, charmingly wrote thanking him for showing her his "private parts". The "stuffed parrot" refers to a cock parrot given by Disraeli to Selina, the third Countess of Bradford, at the turn of the century. The bird, now perched resplendently in Weston, apparently died of shock after laying a single egg on each of 23 days on the trot. (1984)

• • •

Words of wisdom, attributed to Eleanor Roosevelt, came from Baroness Newlove in a Lords debate on international women's day. "A woman is like a teabag," she said. "You can't tell how strong she is until you put her in hot water." (2016)

• • •

The similarities between the late Geoffrey Howe and Lionel Richie are not instantly obvious, but Robin Cook once came up with one. Having been given a title when her husband was knighted and again when he became a peer, Elspeth Howe finally got one of her own when she became a baroness in 2001. Cook observed that this made her "once, twice, three times a lady". (2015)

It is not often that a member of the great Cecil family is almost floored in the course of debate in the House of Lords. But on Wednesday evening, towards the end of the battle over Rhodesian sanctions, Lord Byers, leader of the Liberal peers, gained the distinction of bringing Lord Salisbury practically to his knees.

Leaping to his feet to refute a quotation by the Liberal leader, Lord Salisbury became hopelessly entangled in the strings and attachments of the hearing aid, which surrounded him. It was only the quick thinking of neighbouring peers that saved this mighty standard-bearer of the Tory right wing from collapsing to the floor. As the helpless Marquess was sliding off the side of his bench, strong arms grabbed him, and returned him to his usual upright and dignified position. Lord Byers was suitably concerned about his adversary's condition. "I do hope the noble Lord has not hanged himself," he said sympathetically. (1968)

• • •

A publisher's correction to the latest edition of *Dod's Parliamentary Companion* reads: "Reference Lord Gibson's biography: for National Front read National Trust." (1978)

• • •

There is no father of the House of Lords, presumably because titular membership is no indication of attendance or activity. Lord Romilly has been a peer for 77 years, since succeeding his father at the age of six in 1905, and has yet to make his maiden speech. Still, today the Earl of Listowel celebrates 50 years' activity in the Upper House. He made his maiden speech on March 15, 1932, presumably from the opposition front bench since he was, at that time, one of only six opposition peers. He still takes an important part, and only last week was presiding on the Woolsack. He was the older brother of the Conservative former minister, Viscount Blakenham, who died a week ago, and is, PHS ventures, the father of the active Lords. (1982)

• • •

That resplendent peacock, Lord St John of Fawsley[47], saw off three muggers in St Petersburg at the weekend by expertly wielding a jar of caviare. Joining the Pushkin celebrations for a week, the chairman of the Royal Fine Art Commission had just come out of Yeliseyev's, the city's equivalent of Fortnum & Mason, and was wandering down Nevsky Prospekt when the rotters struck.

"I felt one coming from behind while I noticed another moving in from the front and a third hovering," he tells me. "I turned with my plastic bag containing the caviare and hit the one behind on the head. As I swung back round, the second robber was caught in the face by the plastic bag rebounding, and the third one got the caviare in the unmentionables.

"All three fled, screaming 'mad English'. I must have looked like a combination of Bruce Lee and Lady Bracknell. Luckily the jar of caviare was unbroken." (1999)

• • •

Lord Kagan who died this week, was an extraordinarily ambitious chess player. So much so, that he had an eclectic selection of chess sets. "He always managed to find a chess set with obscure-looking pieces which his opponent couldn't recognise. That gave him a head start," says a regular combatant. "And if that didn't work he would sing loudly in Lithuanian, which would put anyone off." (1995)

---

47 Flamboyant arts minister under Margaret Thatcher.

Members of the House of Lords are far from happy at the fix they have been put in by the government. Today the Commons rises for the summer recess. But peers have two more working days ahead before they adjourn and they are being recalled for a spell in September as well as in October before the new session begins. The avalanche of legislation which has descended on them this month has brought protests from all sides.

It has, I believe, already led to the Leader of the House, Lord Jellicoe, making representations to the government to start more legislation in the Lords next session – a practice which successive governments have been reluctant to follow. A final straw for the over-burdened peers has been the closing of their dining room for the building of an extension. They are having to eat in the Cholmondeley Room. The shortage of space means that not only are guests banned – even for a cup of tea – but some peers, it is whispered have at times had to employ their laps as tables. Politics can be hell. (1972)

"I'm not giving you anything, but
I'll make a cheque out to
the RSPCA."

ANIMALS

Rehearsals of the Regents Park Open Air Theatre production of *A Midsummer Night's Dream*, which opened last night, were enlivened by Bernard Bresslaw's impersonation of the ass. As Bottom, his braying is so lifelike that excited answering calls from the nearby zoo have been clearly heard in the auditorium. Naturalists in the corpsing cast are convinced, however, that the love-lorn responses emanate from the gibbon cage. (1986)

• • •

A story from the Finance Bill committee proceedings, told by Mr John Peyton, Conservative MP for Yeovil: "I heard about a gentleman who was employed in the Treasury, much concerned with principles of national growth – so much so that some therapy was necessary. He bought, or was given, a small dachshund puppy. But after six months, having been the slave of this puppy – he fed it himself morning and night, and he weighed it morning and night – he eventually found himself forced to sell it. He confessed to a colleague that he had done so because, having observed the way the dog had grown, he had come to the conclusion after six months that in another three or four years this tiny little dachshund would be 53 feet long and weigh seven hundredweights. That shows how much he was addicted to the extrapolation of statistics." (1968)

• • •

Roger Mosey, former BBC bigwig, has not been master of Selwyn College, Cambridge, for all that long but he has already broken one of its rules. Mosey writes in the *New Statesman* that he has acquired a basset hound called YoYo but, technically, animals are banned in college, save for the master being allowed to keep a cat. Mosey had to persuade the college council that the dogged YoYo was, in fact, "a very large cat". Albeit one that barks. (2014)

Humphrey the Downing Street cat is missing, presumed dead. He was until recently as familiar at No 10 as John Major, but the black and white tom has been absent since July. Yesterday the Cabinet Office finally lifted its news blackout on the disappearance of an institution. "We fear the worst," said Tim Hunt, the cat's press spokesman. "I think it was his kidneys and he just went away to die." He had recently celebrated his seventh birthday.

Humphrey had been placed on a special diet by his vet after kidney trouble two years ago, aggravated by too many biscuits at elevenses. He recovered, however, and soon afterwards was accused of snatching ducklings from the pond in St James's Park. Some time later, he was reported to have raided a robin's nest in the garden of No 10. Downing Street issued a formal denial to put an end to the "scurrilous" rumours.

John Major was fond of the cat but questioned its sex during a speech at the Conservative Party's Summer Ball last year. Humphrey, he suggested, could well be Henrietta – a confusion that may have arisen because the animal, of dubious parentage, had long since been neutered. The Cabinet Office says that Humphrey had been off his food when last seen – another "top cat" had, after all, arrived in Downing Street in the form of Michael Heseltine. Staff are now steeling themselves to declare Humphrey officially dead, although they are hoping against hope that he might reappear. "I don't dare put a final obituary out," sobbed Tim Hunt.[48] (1995)

---

[48] The disappearance of Humphrey made front-page news. He was eventually found at the Royal Army Medical College. Two years later, there were stories that Tony Blair, the new prime minister, wanted to get rid of Humphrey because his wife disliked cats. Humphrey moved in with an elderly couple in suburban London in November 1997. He died in 2006.

Ian Paisley and Gerry Adams have at last found common cause – a mounting distrust of Peter Mandelson's cherished labrador, Bobby. The reason for their shared animus, I can disclose, stems from the Northern Ireland secretary's habit – some might describe it as a killer strategy – of introducing the dog whenever debates about the peace process overheat. Mandy did this the other day when he met a truculent delegation from Mr Paisley's Democratic Unionist Party, cutting them off mid-rant with the words "Have you met Bobby?" No sooner had he said this than up jumped the Bobster, tail a-wagging. The Orangeman, I am told, was momentarily disarmed.

Mr M appears to have deployed the same tactic with the Sinn Fein leader, who was recently heard to remark, none too quietly, that he was "sick of that f•••••• Bobby." "It is a great way of defusing things, a Northern Ireland source tells me. "Bobby, you could say, is playing a vital part in the peace process." (2000)

• • •

Dogs are to bound on to London's diplomatic stage with a garden party in honour of the furry friends of ambassadors to the Court of St James's. The tea is to be served by the Czech Ambassador, Pavel Seifter, celebrating the release of his beloved 11-year-old grey schnauzer, Cutty, who has just endured six months' hard biscuits in quarantine. Dogs and their guests will be entertained next months with games such as "sniff out their hidden microphone" and a beauty contest to find Miss Jailhouse '98. However, racing will not be allowed because the Czech ambassador's garden is too short.

Joining their excellencies and their canines will be Chris Patten, the former Governor of Hong Kong, who became a determined opponent of the quarantine laws after he was forced to leave his Norfolk terriers,

Whiskey and Soda, in France rather than consign them to six months in the clink. Cutty will be joined by another diplomatic sort's pal, Eddie the French bulldog, with whom it is suggested that Cutty improved international relations during their incarceration.

Students of national traits will be watching the garden party with interest. Will the German ambassador bring a Rottweiler; the French a poodle; the Mexicans a Chihuahua; the Swiss a St Bernard; the Japanese a shihtzu? "We hope to have doggy drinks and bake special biscuits in the shape of bones," says a large plumed hat. "Our only concern is whether there are enough trees for our guests." (1998)

• • •

David Blunkett's guide-dog, Offa, who seems to have staged more farewells than Frank Sinatra, is finally to be let off his lead. After a six-year-parliamentary career, Offa bow-wows out today after listening to questions to the health minister, Virginia Bottomley, and the prime minister.

Long gone are the days when the Alsatian-cross-retriever would steal the show by barking – or occasionally scratching – his response to some point with which he disagreed. Nowadays, old parliamentary paw that he is, he prefers to sleep stretched out on the green carpet, oblivious of the mayhem around him. He retires to live with the vet who treated him for stomach torsions two years ago. "I'll miss him very much," sighs Blunkett, the shadow education secretary. "Listening to the debates in the Commons is hard enough work for me, but it's even harder for Offa." (1994)

A Rottweiler had a narrow escape yesterday when it bit the combative Tory backbencher Anthony Beaumont-Dark in a London park. The dog was enjoying an innocent stroll through Westminster's Embankment Gardens when it was provoked by the sight of the outspoken MP and forced to sink its teeth into Beaumont-Dark's left thigh. It could have been worse; Beaumont-Dark has a metal hip-joint which, fortunately for the poor brute, it missed. Labour MPs, who have been similarly provoked by Beaumont-Dark, were last night said to be preparing a get well card – and alleged to be unsure whether to send it to limping MP or dog. (1990)

. . .

Professor Francois Delaby, a French animal psychiatrist, has produced a novel method of improving the laying productivity of chickens. Delaby was called in last year by the Farming Society of Villepasson to investigate a decrease in laying locally. He decided that the decrease was caused by "a phenomenon of anguish" caused by pigeons from a nearby dovecote. In short, the chickens were jealous of the pigeons' flying ability; or, as Delaby expresses it, experienced "a syndrome of frustrating fixation". He recommended artificial altitude treatment for the chickens. They are suspended from balloons for up to two hours a day each. Productivity is booming, and Delaby is now considering industrial applications of his process. (1969)

"Stay back! It's the work of the Surreal IRA!"

SPEAKING COLLECTIVELY

In 2015, we ran a series on collective nouns, inviting readers to send in their favourites. These included…

After I wrote that the collective noun for a group of news anchors was "an ego", DR Thorpe emailed with a tale about Maurice Bowra, the late warden of Wadham College, Oxford, who once hosted a reception for Charlie Chaplin at which most of the other heads of college were present. When asked what a collective noun would be for such an august body, Bowra suggested: "A lack of principals."

. . .

I have had lots of suggestions from readers of collective nouns for ladies of the night. It all depends on their clients, I suspect. Bakers refer to them as a jam of tarts, while musicians prefer a fanfare of strumpets and bookworms like a novel of trollopes. Literary critics, on the other hand, might prefer an anthology of English pros.

. . .

Dozens of ideas for collective nouns have come in. Mervyn Wigg suggests an amalgam of dentists and Suzie Marwood offers a dislocation of hipsters, but today's favourite is from Billie Pearce, who says that a group of unsuccessful dieters is "an error of their weighs".

. . .

I also received a collective noun from Sophie Neville, who played Titty in the 1974 film of *Swallows and Amazons*. "A gulp of swallows," she suggests, although that reminds me of the adapted proverb, I think by Willie Rushton, that "one swallow does not make an orgy".

More collective nouns have come in: Robert Cobb suggests "a shaft of lawyers", while Clive Coates, who used to work in the police, offers "a thicket of constables" and "an indecision of inspectors". And to prove that we don't censor criticism of ourselves, here's one from Conan Carey: "A scurril of journalists".

• • •

Lots of entries have come in for our new series on collective nouns. Mace Carnochan defines a group of smokers forced to indulge their habit in the open air as "a pack of snoutcasts". Sue Duys recalls working at Wells Cathedral when a group of senior clergy from other cathedrals visited. She suggested they should be known as a Forest of Deans.

BARRY FANTONI

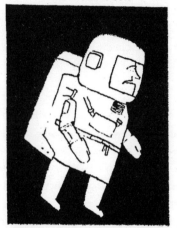

"Hullo, Houston control – I've just
been mugged"

EXPLORERS

Conqueror of the Arctic ice, climber of Everest, victim of a toilet door. At a Mumm champagne launch at Wellington Arch yesterday Bear Grylls, the intrepid British explorer and former member of the SAS, confessed that the unremarkable trip down from Wales had almost defeated him. "I was stuck in the loo on the train," he said. "I had to be rescued by a rather indignant old lady." (2006)

. . .

The evenings can drag when you are trekking across a polar ice shelf. In a talk at the How:to Academy, Sir Ranulph Fiennes said that his favourite way of passing the time was to play Boggle, the dice-based letters game. On one expedition, though, space in the bags was at a premium. "So we played chess," he said, "using urine bottles collected by the expedition doctor. Those with blue caps for one player and those with red caps for the other." Presumably pawns could be taken "en pissant". (2015)

. . .

Mitzi McCall, the widow of Scottish artist Charles McCall, only opened an exhibition of her husband's work this week. She regaled guests with tales of her husband's early struggles to sell paintings. "When we first moved to Tite Street in the 1950s it was difficult to sell a picture, so we rented out rooms. We had artists and sculptors everywhere." One lodger was not part of the artistic community. "In 1954, a New Zealander rented out the top floor. He had to leave because he said he couldn't cope with the rickety staircase. His name was Edmund Hillary. The year before he had climbed Everest." (1992)

Some adventurers bring back perfume from their travels as a gift for the wife. Sir David Attenborough told the *Radio Times* festival that he once returned from the jungle with a couple of bush babies. God knows how he got them through customs — "These short, hairy creatures? They're my researchers" — but he took them home, where they swiftly climbed the curtains and urinated on the settee. Unfortunately, the Attenboroughs had guests over for dinner that evening and one lady's nostril started twitching as soon as she arrived. "I could see her thinking, 'That's not mulligatawny soup'," Attenborough said. (2015)

• • •

Attenborough often struggles with re-entry into domestic life. On one return from Borneo, he woke at 2am dripping with sweat and assumed the worst. "I thought, 'This is it, this is malarial fever'," he said. It was only in the morning that he discovered his wife had bought an electric blanket while he was away. (2015)

• • •

Lord Healey, the former Chancellor and author of every kind of book from *The Race Against the H Bomb* to *When Shrimps Learn to Whistle*, is in publishing mood once again. His latest departure is *Healey's World*, in which he becomes a bushy-eyebrowed Alan Whicker and displays his photograph collection – largely pictures of his wife, Edna, posing demurely in a variety of terrains. On one of his trips to Borneo, however, he relates a story of how he indulged in a binge of drinking "tuak" (cider, honey and gin) and taking part in a sword dance.

"Edna performed so well that the head man gestured for a large rope net to be lowered from the rafters," he reveals. "Out of it rolled a number of small wicker baskets about the size of small melons. The head man picked one out and presented it to Edna. It contained the head of a Japanese soldier, perfectly preserved by being hung in the smoke of a fire. On returning to London we declared the head to customs as an anthropological specimen. It lay in a plastic bag behind the sofa in our bedroom at Admiralty House until found by a woman cleaner, who took a long time to recover." (2002)

. . .

John Simpson, the BBC world affairs editor, was not given the reception he expected when he returned to see his English tutor, Arthur Sale. Interviewed in *CAM*, the magazine for Cambridge alumni, he revealed that he went back after a particularly scary tour of duty in Afghanistan which included a piece to camera as fighting went on around him. Sale chastised him: "You split two infinitives when the guns were going off." (2003)

. . .

Sir Ranulph Fiennes, the arctic explorer, has been ordered by the Cub Scouts Association to retake his tent-making badge. The humiliating blow follows claims by his second cousin, the artist Susannah Fiennes, that Sir Ranulph failed to build her an adequate shelter while she painted his Exmoor home. "He tried to build me a shelter, but all his arctic skills were to no avail," Susannah reveals. The Cub Association is firm but fair. "We can't withdraw his badge, but we can retrain him." (1999)

Brooke Shields's bid to escape the unwanted attentions of the opposite sex by taking an Arctic Circle holiday have backfired. The comely actress, who has been the victim of a stalker in Los Angeles, had sought some rare privacy with her new squeeze Chris Henchy in the comfort of an igloo in the icy outposts of northern Canada. Sadly, their plans fell foul of an indigenous Eskimo custom. "If a male member of the Inuit people seeks refuge in your igloo, it's customary to offer him clothing, food and your woman," warns Shields. "All the Inuits asked Chris where our igloo was so they could 'drop by'. I slept with a metal rod by my side just in case." (2000)

"At least this train runs on time."

PLANES, TRAINS AND AUTOMOBILES

First TransPennine Express has sent me a list of unusual objects in its Lost Property Office. It includes 3kg of haggis, 16 inflatable dolls, a suitcase filled with taxidermied rats and an unused ticket for the Olympic 100m sprint final. If they all belonged to the same person that sounds like one hell of a party he misplaced. (2013)

• • •

How to beat a random breathalyser test. A reader was stopped while driving his British-bought right-hand-drive Citroen in France last summer. A bag was automatically passed through the left-hand window. The front seat passenger blew into it and handed it back. Result: negative. The officer waved them on. Moral: buy a left-hand-drive Metro. (1981)

• • •

Amber Rudd, the energy secretary, has had a train named after her in her constituency of Hastings. It's called the Amber Rudd Seaside Express, although she was less than chuffed when a ticket inspector told her that they like to shorten it to Arse. (2016)

• • •

Of all the jobs in politics, that of Conservative transport secretary must have the shortest lifespan. Since 1964, 17 Tories have run the department but, assuming he doesn't get run over by a battlebus in the next three days, Patrick McLoughlin will displace Nicholas Ridley as the one with the most time at the wheel in the past 50 years. Transport can be a soul-destroying brief. Labour's Alistair Darling was asked what he learnt from almost four years in the post. Darling replied: "To drive at 69.5mph for hours at a time." (2015)

The £100m rebuilding programme at Gatwick airport is now nearing completion but I gather that moves, first made three years ago, to change its name to Winston Churchill International are still unlikely to succeed. The British Airports Authority, impressed by the charisma of Charles de Gaulle International airport and John F Kennedy International airport – both affectionately known by their initials – are less keen on "WC International". (1978)

• • •

Sir Thomas Sopwith, whose Hampshire estate is for sale at £15 million, was an intrepid balloonist, aviator and yachtsman, but he took parental fright at his son Tommy's desire to become a racing driver. Tommy recalls reminding his father of the many times the old man had crashed aeroplanes. "Yes", replied Sopwith senior, but we crashed so slowly". (1989)

• • •

A nice line from Lord Adonis, the former transport secretary, when talking about rail links across the north: "Apart from my own name, the Transpennine Express is the greatest misnomer of all time." (2014)

• • •

A friend was on a No 38 bus recently travelling west, when a passenger asked the West Indian conductor whether this bus was right for Victoria. Yes, lady," he replied. She then turned to her female neighbour, and, thinking the conductor could not hear, said: "Is this bus right for Victoria, do you know?" Yes," said the other lady. The conductor, however, had heard both the repeated question and the answer. "There, lady, now you have it in black and white," he said. (1967)

Downing Street, I'm told, rang Lord King, chairman of British Airways, on Friday and said: "We want somebody to come to dinner on Monday night with the prime minister of India." Lord King expressed regret, saying he would be away on business on the US. "No, no, not you," came the reply. "We want an ordinary pilot who can talk to him about something he knows about." (1985)

• • •

Customer care, British Airways style. A plumpish woman complained to staff on BA's Bournemouth stand about the size of their seats: "They are too small. Can't you make them a little bigger?" she asked. "No madam, we can't," the heartless stewardess replied. "However, we do serve low-calorie meals." (1999)

• • •

We've parked our rented Ford Focus next to the Palais des Festivals in Cannes (because Jack refused to be seen in public climbing out of it in his black tie) and noted that the floor we were on was called "Niveau James Dean". "Hmmmm," said Jack. "A man killed in a car crash to help you remember where you parked your car. Do you think the other levels are named after Ayrton Senna, Marc Bolan and Princess Grace? Maybe we'll be flying home from Buddy Holly Airport." (2001)

• • •

Virgin Atlantic and British Airways are squabbling over BA's slogan "The world's favourite airline". Virgin was the only British airline in the top notch in a recent passenger survey and Richard Branson, the carrier's boss, is now planning his own advertising campaign hijacking the slogan. BA claims its line refers to the volume of passengers. "We carry more international passengers than any other world airline," says a spokesman. Virgin is unimpressed. "By that logic, the M25 is the world's favourite motorway". (1991)

• • •

The train strikes have meant slow business for Buster Edwards, the 63-year-old former great train robber who has served his term for the £2.6 million heist and now sells flowers outside Waterloo station. "We only stopped one train – not all of them," he complains. "Now it looks like they're getting me back. You could say it's poetic justice." (1994)

• • •

With renewed doubts about the ability of airport security machines to detect plastic explosives, a *Times* journalist recalls a visit to Morocco last year. At Tangier airport, departing for home, he realised that two antique silver pistols bought in the town were packed in the suitcase that was, at that moment, passing through the X-ray machine. Fearing that he was about to set off a security alert, he confessed his foolishness to a guard. "Don't worry, sir," came the reply. "Our machines will never pick them up." We are reliably told they are now much more efficient. (1991)

• • •

Part of the April Fool's day was spent worrying about Mrs Schilling's letter to *The Times* in which she suggests that Ladies Only compartments are the answer to sexual assaults on the railway. If a man is seen to approach, she argues, pull the communication cord. With some 15 per cent of the population short-sighted, non-English-reading or illiterate there would be an unprecedented number of tugs at the cord, and even more delays to trains than we currently enjoy. Perhaps a Rapists Only compartment ... but again there is the problem of literacy. (1988)

• • •

A new game at Orly airport: early this week crowds going up to the first floor had a choice: the main staircase or the escalator, which was out of action. Many people chose the immobile escalator, which was neither working nor anchored. When there were enough people on it, it started moving ... downward; the faster people ran towards the top, the faster it went ... downwards. When they were safely back where they started (helped by watchers in hysterics) all was well for a few more moment until a further crowd arrived and again chose the escalator. The pleasant scene was repeated a number of times before the authorities intervened. (1971)

"It symbolises his reluctance to have £114,000 a year and a flat overlooking the Thames"

WHITEHALL

As impatience turns to anger over the delay in publishing the Chilcot report into the Iraq war, *Civil Service World* has provided a timely guide to when you should expect reports to be published relative to their promised date. If you are told "in the new year", expect it at Easter; spring means "by the summer recess", summer means "by mid-October" and autumn naturally means "by Christmas". The killer, though, is "in due course". This is Whitehall code for "I have no idea when — or if — we will publish this". (2015)

• • •

Nice to know that taxpayer money is being spent wisely by the Department for Education. A parliamentary written answer reveals that £6,167 was spent at the World Professional Darts Championships "to encourage darts fans to phone the National Learning Advice and find out about courses to improve their maths and English skills". Darts fans may be incensed by the implication that they need help. (2005)

• • •

Time stood still in Whitehall yesterday. The department of environment have hitherto retained the services of two clock-winders to keep the clock-work ticking over. Yesterday the retirement of one coincided with the sickness of the other so everything stopped. Just about teatime, as it happens. (1976)

• • •

Today's entry in our series on decoding civil service jargon comes from Don Grubin, who compares when officials in the home office say that something will happen and when it does. "'Quickly' = two weeks," he says. "'Almost there' = four. 'As fast as humanly possible' = nine. 'By the summer' = before the end of November. 'It will take a while' = never."

Even their job titles need decoding. Sir Bob Kerslake, the former chief mandarin, tells *Civil Service World* about being asked for his job title when he bought a flat recently. "Permanent secretary," he replied. "Secretary? That's a good job," the estate agent replied. "And isn't it great they've made it permanent?" (2015)

• • •

Andrew Parker, chief spook at MI5, insists that James Bond was never representative of the secret service. At an event in the City, he read a memo from 1953, when *Casino Royale* was published, in which a new spy was told that "one of the best things about working here is that the percentage of bastards is extremely low". Someone should commission a new study: which Whitehall department has the lowest bastard quotient? (2015)

• • •

A service of thanksgiving for the work of HM Revenue and Customs was held at Westminster Abbey last week. The creative organisers chose "Lo the poor crieth" as the psalm, took a reading from Corinthians that says "God loves a cheerful giver" and included a reminder in the prayers that it is more blessed to give than receive. (2014)

• • •

At last, an explanation for falling classroom standards. Predictably, it's Balls. Apparently, every time the schools secretary sends out a vital Whitehall edict in his name, the message is automatically blocked by the nation's censorious school software programmes.

"I appreciate that schools don't want to encourage the use of what they see as 'bad words'," says Tony Attwood, editor of the Schools Directory newsletter. "But I am not sure that exposure to the minister's name is going to harm anyone in the communications technology services department."

We invited the minister to lance this boil and choose a nom de plume more suited to a future leadership candidate, Obama, perhaps? Or even his wife's sensible name, Cooper? "We don't know anything about IT," says his press office. "We don't know anything." Somehow, this seems entirely believable. (2008)

• • •

There was hollow laughter at the British Tourist Authority's information centre in St James's when a call came from the department of trade to say that a group of visiting dignitaries were expected and could the centre provide the comprehensive information packs which had been so much appreciated in the past. The centre closed yesterday, as part of budget cuts ordered by the department of trade. (1983)

• • •

The Tories are fond of attacking Labour's profligacy in office, but there was one area in which money was saved. When Ed Balls left the Treasury in 2004 after seven years as Gordon Brown's henchman, his secretary made a confession. "You know every day you've had a tray, which has two bottles of Malvern water on it?" she told him. "Well, every morning, I'd fill the bottles from the tap." Balls tells *The House* magazine that a senior civil servant had told her that ministers really didn't need mineral water, especially not the Queen's favourite brand. A fagpacket calculation suggests that Julie, the secretary, saved the nation about £3,000 doing this. Maybe she should be chancellor (2014)

A press notice from the department of transport tells me that the secretary of state, Norman Fowler, has significantly reduced the number of circulars his department send out to local authorities. Such waste-cutting is most commendable, but did they really need to send us four copies of the notice? (1981)

• • •

Andrew Gray of the University of Kent tells a jolly Civil Service tale, which I enjoy even if I do not altogether believe it. A certain permanent secretary retired to a small West Country village, where he moved into an old-world cottage in the main street. After a while his neighbours noticed that early every morning a young boy would knock on his door, exchange a few words with the retired mandarin, accept a tip, and go on his way.

After several weeks observing this practice; the curiosity of the villagers got the better of them, and they questioned the youth. "Tell us," they urged, "Why do you always knock on the old man's door in the morning? And what do you say to each other? And why does he pay you?"

"Well," replied the youth, "It's a bit odd. The old man pays me ten pence every morning if I knock on his door and tell him the minister wants to see him." "And what does he reply?" they asked. "Tell the minister to •••• off ," said the youth. (1981)

• • •

Rigorous steps are being taken in the campaign to curb farmers' subsidies. Staff at the ministry of agriculture have made four separate applications for new stock of ballpoint pens, and each has been met with a hand-written (so someone's got some) refusal. It is impossible to sign ministry cheques without a pen. Admirably simple tactics, Mrs Thatcher. (1984)

• • •

So much for open government. Ringing the office of the parliamentary commissioner, a colleague asked the official he spoke to for his name (not for use but purely in case of query). The official refused. "Who can I say I was talking to then?" "The office of the parliamentary commissioner." This is the office which is supposed to look after a citizen's grievances against an increasingly remote, impersonal bureaucracy. (1972)

THE LAST POST

The Post Office does not change. The *Ripon Gazette and Observer* reports: "The building up of long queues at Ripon Post Office during the lunch hour, which has brought many complaints from customers may be solved by closing the building during this peak period." (1977)

• • •

When councillors at Wadebridge in Cornwall wanted to object to the planned closure of the sub-post office at the nearby village of Egloshyle, they sent a protest letter to the main PO at Truro. Instead of carrying an Egloshyle postmark, it was delivered by hand. "We didn't trust the postal service," said the mayor, Hyacinth Varcoe. (1984)

• • •

Anna Freud, the youngest child of Sigmund and a distinguished psychoanalyst in her own right, lived on the west coast of Cork at the end of her life. She was in Skibereen for her 70th birthday and received hundreds of telegrams of goodwill from all parts of the world. The messages were telephoned through to the postmistress, who inscribed them on greeting forms and hired a boy to deliver them hourly to the Freud house. During the afternoon she received one which read: "The rapists of Philadelphia send good wishes and best regards." This puzzled Dr Freud greatly. When she called on the postmistress the next day she asked if she might send off for verification. It turned out that "therapists" is not a word in common usage around those parts. (1988)

• • •

When Harold and Mary Wilson moved into Lord North Street they were given a private telephone number. This week a friend, wanting to speak to Mary Wilson, phoned that number and was surprised to find herself talking to Conservative Central Office. At first she suspected a sensational defection from the Labour camp, but she discovered that the Wilsons' number had simply been changed. The Post Office often change the private numbers of the famous if they become too widely known and reallocate the old number elsewhere. Whether this particular switch was accidental or effected by a wag with a taste for the ridiculous is not known. (1975)

• • •

The Israel post office has decided to withdraw a stamp bearing the name of God following complaints from religious circles that to destroy, lick or frank it was a sin. The stamp, one of a series issued to commemorate the Jewish New Year, showed the synagogue of Tunis with the Hebrew four letter name of God clearly visible on the stained glass window. Since destruction of the stamp is a sin, remaining stocks will stay forever in the post office vaults. (1970)

• • •

Among the congratulatory telegrams sent to Hugh Cudlipp about his knighthood was one from members of the National Union of Journalists at the Manchester office of the *Daily Mirror*. It read: "A rise, Sir Hugh?" (1973)

• • •

The letter was addressed to A. Carnegie, Esq., Moodie Street, Dunfermline, Fife, Scotland. It contained a missive from Encyclopaedia Britannica International Ltd, beginning: "Good morning. Thank you for your enquiry ... in response we have pleasure in enclosing our descriptive booklet..." Unfortunately for the Britannica, Carnegie left the Moodie Street address for the United States in 1848. Thus Brian

Blench, director of museums of the Carnegie Dunfermline Trust, which includes the Moodie Street cottage, has pointed out to the Britannica that if Carnegie did inquire from that address for information as they suggest in their opening sentence, the letters have taken 123 years to accomplish their journey. (1971)

• • •

You may not believe this, but the British Post Office has just won an award in New York. Not, sadly, for its impeccable service, but for being especially cooperative towards the philatelic press. Alex Currall, the managing director, could not get to the award ceremony, but sent a message of thanks. Luckily, it arrived in time. (1973)

• • •

Tax inspectors do not always demand money with menaces. Trevor Boucher, Australia's Commissioner for Taxation, has just sent a 100th birthday telegram to Leslie Muir of Canberra congratulating him on joining the select group of centenarian tax-payers. "Your contribution in revenue in over 75 years of diligent tax payment is greatly appreciated. My staff join me in the fond hope that many years of life and taxes lie ahead of you." (1990)

• • •

It must be obvious to all who write letters to *The Times* that more are received than can be printed. This sad fact had not escaped the eagle eye of the late Colonel Wintle. From the Cavalry Club in 1946 he sent this to the Editor. "Sir – I have just written you a long letter. On reading it over, I have thrown it into the wastepaper basket. Hoping this will meet with your approval. I am, Sir, your obedient servant, A. D. Wintle." (1966)

*"I'm not saying he's paranoid,
but it's the only ministerial
desk with wing mirrors."*

AND FINALLY ...

Joan Rivers, the vinegar-tongued comedian, who died last year, is to be honoured at a glitzy gala tonight by her alma mater, Barnard College in Manhattan, against opposition from some academics who found her humour too filthy. Rivers, who graduated in English in 1954, addressed the 50-year reunion and said: "Remember, it's not who you know — it's whom." Apparently only half of the alumni got the joke. (2015)

. . .

Two young punk females overheard on top of a 19 bus this week. First YPF: "I'm thinking of getting meself a job. What about you?" Second YPF: "Oh no, I've got very old-fashioned ideas about a girl going out to work. I think she should be on social security". (1980)

. . .

The ICA seeks volunteers to re-enact the mass suicide at Jonestown 21 years ago. Rod Dickinson, an "artist and crop-circle maker", wants to recreate the last hours of Rev Jim Jones's crowd in Guyana where 914 people died after taking potassium cyanide. The re-enactment will be helped by tapes from survivors. The Live Arts Department is distributing enticing leaflets: "Would you like to take part?" (1999)

. . .

It must be hard to feel nostalgia for a prison camp, but there will be few dry eyes around when the PoW elite of the Second World War meet in London today for a Colditz reunion. Earl Haig (son of the First World War commander-in-chief), who was incarcerated in Colditz from November 1944 until being liberated by the Russians in April 1945, says that after so many years, recognition of fellow prisoners has become a problem at reunions. "Everyone looks so different that it takes until the end of the party to recognise old friends. Then I want to discuss old wounds, pleasures and memories, but it's too late. You end up regretting you can't be back in Colditz with them all." (1990)

• • •

When Douglas Hogg, the agriculture secretary, met Franz Fischler, the EU agriculture commissioner, in Brussels last week, he was among friends, thanks to his adroit adviser, George Osborne. Fischler, a jovial Austrian, visited London in February for talks with Hogg. After lunch, however, he found himself at a loose end for the afternoon. Osborne, 24, suggested a visit to the Cezanne exhibition at the Tate. Fischler looked excited. Tickets, however, would be harder to come by than an EU cow-slaughtering grant.

A call was put through to the department of national heritage. No dice. Re-enter Osborne. Producing a Friends of the Tate card, he ventured that if he could get the commissioner in as a guest on his card, his chef de cabinet could probably sneak in as well. So, taking the chance, they headed off. The plan was smoother than the chef de cabinet's hair grease. While Osborne signed Fishcler in as his guest, Le Chef darted past the distracted security staff and into the show. The Austrians were said to be highly impressed.[49] (1996)

---

[49] This was the first mention of George Osborne in the Diary. He was elected to Parliament in 2001 and became chancellor of the exchequer just before his 39th birthday.

A Conversation with Oscar Wilde, the Maggi Hambling sculpture near Trafalgar Square, is again missing its bronze cigarette. It has been sawn off and replaced several times since the statue was installed in 1998. Noting this, the actor Sir Ian McKellen said: "How far we've travelled when Wilde is reviled not for being gay, but for being a smoker." (2014)

• • •

A sharp dispute has arisen between the leading auction houses and the Victoria & Albert Museum. It concerns the latter's cricket team, which is alleged to be full of ringers. The V & A recently played Sotheby's and hammered them. Tomorrow they meet Christie's and the antecedents of their team will be closely scrutinized. "It is no good playing febrile types who turn out in Fiorucci track suits and stand on the boundary remarking the too, too Turneresque sky, oblivious to the ball flying past them," says the V & A's captain, Nicky Bird. "Our players all have a connexion with the museum. Our opening bowler, for example, sheltered in the doorway during a shower. We feel it is not how you play the game, but whether you win or lose." (1983)

• • •

Sir William Black, chairman of the National Research Development Corporation, has a cautionary tale showing how even the best brains can go sadly wrong once they stray outside their accustomed disciplines. A brilliant young scientist colleague, he says, discovered a promising artist whose paintings he both liked and thought might prove a good investment. He bought one or two and was gratified some months later to discover that the man's prices had risen. He engaged an agent to look out for canvases and buy them, and soon afterwards asked another dealer to do the same. Prices continued to rise. It was not until 18 months later that he discovered he was his protégé's only buyer. Prices had been inflated because his two agents were bidding one against the other. (1968)

Harrods is facing unexpected criticism from patrons over its black-and-white, closed-circuit television security system. A titled Knightsbridge lady has been heard to say to another as they caught a glimpse of the inside of a security room: "One might expect Harrods to show their customers in colour!" (1981)

. . .

Christmas is a magical time for Brian Cox, who goes to extreme lengths to make Santa's visit more memorable for his two children. "I like making reindeer poo," the astrophysicist tells *Time Out*. "You have to mix Nutella and peanut butter to create the idea of incontinent reindeer." As a child Cox loved to appear in Nativity plays. "I was always a Wise Man because I could point so well," he says. "Though I would get told off when I explained the astronomical errors in the tale of them following the star." (2013)

. . .

Jeffrey Archer is running his first marathon at the age of 64 to try to raise £1.6million for charity, beating the £1,126,560 record for any one individual. The money will be handled by the Charities Aid Foundation. Archer's appeal letter, which he sent to his friends, signs off: "Would you be kind enough to support me by filling in the sponsorship form – and then add a nought to the figure you first thought of." (2004)

. . .

Inflation note: Asked by a small boy for a penny for his guy, a colleague in south London explained that he had only a £5 note. "That's all right", replied the lad, diving into a coin-crammed pocket. "I can change it." (1976)

The English Tourist Board's publication *England* gives a dampening indication of the sort of welcome you might get if you holiday in this country. The cover shows a young couple looking pleased with themselves in a boat, and inside a note says the picture was taken at Castle Howard, adding: "Please note that boating facilities are not available to the public." (1976)

. . .

The secretary to the dean of Divinity at Magdalen College, Oxford, wrote to a student to say he was on the list to read the first lesson at evensong. "Please let me know", he added cautiously, "if you are not able to read." (1975)

. . .

Despite its somewhat melodramatic title, Mr Gordon Rattray Taylor (former editor of the BBC TV science series *Horizon*) believes his forthcoming book *The Biological Time-Bomb* understates rather than exaggerates the likely advances in our ability to preserve the human body and brain. It will be published next month by Thames and Hudson. "I've left out things I considered far-fetched and mentioned only what seems reasonably likely," he says. Among developments he considers probable before the year 2000 are: the power to postpone death indefinitely; to modify the mind by drugs, erase and edit memory and regulate desire; to modify heredity and enhance the intelligence of offspring; and the creation of chimeras such as monkeys with human hands and enhanced intelligence. Bred perhaps as helots to work in factories. (1968)

Dr Robert Brenner, deputy director of the United States National Highway Safety Bureau, yesterday gave his own version of the phrase: "There are honest men, liars and statisticians." He said at the US embassy in London: "A statistician is a man with one foot in a hot frying pan, the other in an ice cube who says 'On average I feel pretty good'." (1970)

. . .

One of the more poignant passages from Andy Warhol's newly published diary concerns a "little freelance" who started crying after the editor of Warhol's magazine rejected one of her fashion stories. Warhol says he thought about hiring her, but decided she did not know how to dress. The lady was Anna Wintour. Nowadays she edits *Vogue* and wears Chanel. (1989)

. . .

Queen Anne is to get her sceptre back, and a new cross for her orb. This will do delayed justice for her statue outside St Paul's. Since the sceptre and cross disappeared after Sir Winston Churchill's funeral, she has had the air of a wicket-keeper appealing to the umpire. The trouble is, say the Corporation of London, she is in a vulnerable position. Like Eros she is inclined to lose things. They are not alone. In Hyde Park Achilles is less in fear of his heel than his fig-leaf.

Like Anne, Queen Victoria in Kensington Gardens suffers from sceptre-snatchers. The Ministry of Public Building and Work say they do not keep spares for dispossessed statues. It means making new parts. They provided Peter Pan with new pipes when he was deprived of his instrumentation. Then the police recovered the old ones. The ministry are hanging on to them. They never know when they will be needed. (1966)

Denis Thatcher may not know it, but a select group of Washington men married to eminent women have made him their spiritual leader. *The Washington Times* exposed the existence of the Denis Thatcher Society last week. Members tend to be known by their wives' names – ie, Mr Constance Horner, husband of the under-secretary of the department of health and human services, or Mr Cathie Black, husband of the publisher of *USA Today*. Membership is said to be "a state of mind". The society's main activities are lunches at Washington club where the men can charge their meals to their wives. (1989)

• • •

Mary Whitehouse is displeased with a four-letter word in her home address. With 14 neighbours at Ardleigh, Essex, she has signed a petition asking the parish council to change the name of their road from Dead Lane to Dede Lane. 'It has always been embarrassing to give my address," she says. "Dede Lane would sound much sweeter." (1983)

• • •

Bare legs are acceptable at Harrods, but midriffs are out. Because of the hot weather the store has "redefined its dress code" – and annoyed a few account holders who, not unreasonably, think they might have been told first. One of the most indignant is a lady of my acquaintance who was refused entry with her daughter because of the girl's cropped cotton blouse. The offending garment had been bought, of course at Harrods. (1989)